Ethics:
Contemporary Perspectives

Text copyright © 2013 remains with the authors and for the collection with ATF Press. All rights reserved. Except for any fair dealing permitted under the Copyright Act, no part of the publication may be reproduced by any means without prior permission. Inquiries should be made in the first instance with the publisher.

Ethics: Contemporary Perspectives
Volume 1, Number 1, 2013

Ethics: Contemporary Perspectives
We live in an evolving and increasingly complex global community and with this complexity comes a broad range of ethical issues. The new interdisciplinary journal, *Ethics: Contemporary Perspectives*, seeks to bring together scholars from across the humanities, social sciences, and sciences, including disciplines as diverse as philosophy, law, medicine and the study of world religions, to discuss these broad ethical issues in contemporary society. A peer reviewed journal, *Ethics* aimed at exploring our complex world, addressing both old and new ethical issues through scholarly discourse.

This is a new, international, interdisciplinary, and refereed journal which is to be published annually by ATF Press in association with the University of Adelaide Research Unit for the Study of Society, Law and Religion (RUSSLR). The publication is both an online and print edition journal. The first issue of the journal has an international line up of leading scholars in a range of disciplines from the USA, Canada, New Zealand, France and Australia. It will address the theme of 'The Ethics of Ethics' and will come out in the first half of 2013. The second edition in 2014 will deal with 'Space Ethics'.

Editor Board
Dr Bernadette Richards, Law School University of Adelaide, Editor in Chief.
Associate Professor Paul Babie, Director, Research Unit for the Study of Society, Law and Religion, University of Adelaide
Professor Robert Crotty, former Director, Ethics Centre of South Australia, Emeritus Professor of Religion and Education, University of South Australia

Business Manager
Mr Hilary Regan, Publisher, ATF Theology, PO Box 504 Hindmarsh, SA 5007, Australia. Fax +61 8 82235643.

Vol 1/ 1 2013

Subscription rates 2013/2014
Print: Local: Individual $Aus55, Institutions Aus$65. **Overseas:** Individuals US$60, Institutions US$65.
OnLine: Local: Individuals $Aus 45, Institutions: Aus $55. **Overseas:** Individuals US$50, Institutions US$60
Print and Online **Local:** Individuals $Aus 65, Institutions Aus$85.
Overseas: Individuals US$70, Institutions US$80.

Ethics: Contemporary Perspectives is published by ATF Theology and imprint of ATF (Australia) Ltd (ABN 90 116 359 963) and is published once a year.
ISSN 2201-3563

Cover design by Astrid Sengkey. Layout/Artwork by Anna Dimasi
Text Minion Pro Size 11

Ethics:
Contemporary Perspectives

The Ethics of Ethics

Table of Contents

Introduction · vii

Vulnerable Human Beings And
'The Canary In The Mine' Principle In Ethics
   Grant Gillett · 1

A Loss Of Faith:
Law, Justice And Legal Ethics
   Allan C Hutchinson · 18

The Genealogy of Space Ethics
   Jacques Arnould · 42

Sigillum Confessionis: The Seal Of
Confession In Today's Roman Catholic Church
   Robert Crotty · 57

Introduction

On behalf of the editorial committee I would like to welcome you to the first edition of *Ethics: Contemporary Perspectives* which focuses on broad questions of the ethics of ethics. We sent out a broad invitation to contribute and received diverse responses which means that this, the first edition, represents an eclectic mix of ideas and issues relating to ethics. There is, however, one unifying theme that runs through the discussions which is fitting for a new journal, crossing the frontier from concept to reality: new frontiers and exploring borders.

In our first piece, 'A Loss of Faith: Law, Justice and Legal Ethics' Prof Allan Hutchinson explores the frontier between ethical, and unethical, lawyering. He cautions that the modern-day lawyer is not perceived as morally or ethically robust and that this is harming the profession. The answer is not, according to Hutchinson, to offer 'better explanations and novel justifications' for existing practices (and here, he refers to the work of Bradley Wendel). Rather, the solution is to change both what lawyers do and how they think about what they do. His discussion calls for a shift into a new frontier which represents a defensible theory of legal ethics which includes an ethical account of ethics.

In our second piece, Prof Grant Gillet, 'Vulnerable human beings and the "canary in the mine" principle in ethics' explores how we think about ethics the human condition. He suggests that marginalised members of society can warn us of practices that are toxic and therefore provide a protective role for the whole of society. Thus the 'canary in the mine' of the title. He explores how we see morality, how we determine what is right and wrong and how we become aware of human-living. The frontier in this piece is that of human interaction and enrichment and a 'simple thesis': 'that the voices of the disadvantaged and marginalised bring to our attention aspects of society that threaten human well-being'.

In our third piece, Dr Jacques Arnauld takes us to the frontier of space and explores the need for an ethics of space exploration. His very interesting discussion explores humanity's yearning for space and the perceived need to step outside of the bounds of earth. He introduces the idea of the expansion of the global village and asks what role ethics has in this expansion. He even goes so far as to ask ought we explore space? This wide-ranging discussion concludes that space, once the forbidden frontier, is now more accessible and more human than ever before. Thus the ethics of expanding humanity must be considered and the expansion into space embraced as representing a 'unique horizon' of ethics which 'concentrates the world to the scale of humanity'.

Our fourth and final piece is a discussion piece exploring the apparently impenetrable frontier of the confessional. There is a clear line drawn in Australia between Church and State and this line is under challenge given the public enquiry into the seal of the confession. Associate Emeritus Professor Robert Cotty explains the history of the seal alongside the Royal Commission. This piece does not provide any suggestions or recommendation, rather it serves as an introduction to the key issues and the 'intractable problem' of the different imperatives behind Church and State actions. It would appear unlikely that the frontier of the confessional seal will be breached.

We are indeed fortunate to have attracted contributors of such calibre and hope that the small but diverse selection of papers is of interest to you. The editorial committee would like to thank our four contributors for welcoming our new journal and being prepared to contribute. We would also like to thank ATF Press and RUSSLR for their support of the journal. And of course, we would like to thank you, the reader, for taking the time to engage with our discussions.

Bernadette Richards
Paul Babie
Robert Crotty

Vulnerable Human Beings And 'The Canary In The Mine' Principle In Ethics

Grant Gillett
University of Otago, Dunedin, New Zealand

This paper outlines a very simple thesis: that the voices of the disadvantaged and marginalised often bring to our attention aspects of society that threaten human well-being or are even toxic to the human spirit. That thesis transforms the ethics of attending to vulnerable human beings—such as those who are differently-abled, the disenfranchised, those who are the underclass and the marginalised—from resting on a poorly articulated sense of human rights or on compassion to being of central importance in discussions about the well-being of all. Rights talk, for instance, is often ungrounded and only rhetorically applicable to certain human contexts if an accompanying set of first world normative assumptions are accepted. Feeling with others or caring about what happens to them may be a basic ingredient of all moralities but also can be critiqued as merely an emotive hangover of our primitive tribal instincts. Such rhetorical or emotive justifications need to be grounded in an analysis of the human condition that makes sense of our reactive attitudes as intrinsic to distinctively human rationality.[1] The appeal could rest on an intuition like, 'There but for the grace of God go I?' Something like a Rawlsian veil of ignorance allows one then to argue for the moral considerations being blind to societal position because any participant in the moral discussion might occupy that position.[2] The Rawlsian model, however, does seem a little too comfortable in its fit with North American liberalism to adequately deal with the protests of the oppressed and

---

1. Strawson, P *Freedom and Resentment and Other Essays* (London: Methuen, 1974).
2. The discounting is based on the plausibility of my being in the unfortunate position of the disadvantaged person who is the mortal patient.

the victims of historical injustice. A global ethics should aim to create a context in which various kinds of human life and commitments are sustainable in a developed world of unprecedented challenges where inequities have been allowed to arise and often are accompanied by a silencing of those who are worst affected.[3]

If we approach the issue through a naturalistic or evolutionary foundation for ethics, the resulting meta-ethical framework has some claim to be widely applicable and also resonates with an approach to human neuro-cognitive function pioneered in the Darwinian period of intellectual ferment. The key thinker in that project is John Hughlings Jackson and his articulation, in the light of clinical neurology, of 'the evolution and dissolution of nervous function' centred on integration and self-coordination.[4] When his approach is spelt out, it implies that there may be a fairly adaptive foundation for an ethics of special concern for the vulnerable and an empathic universalisability (a kind of 'warm Kantianism' based on 'a kingdom of ends'). On the view suggested, differently abled and marginalised people have vulnerabilities that are endemic in all human beings and when they find practices and discourses around them to be toxic we should all take notice and use that insight to help fashion sustainable modes of living together.

Vulnerable Human Beings and Marginalisation.

Vulnerable human beings are often marginalised and effectively silenced as a moral and political voice in public debate. Such silences arise in two general ways: either because of factors within the person of which he or she may be unaware but which have an ongoing effect on his or her voice; or because of things that the person is aware of but for which s/he cannot find appropriate words in the permitted discourse of engagement. The latter tends to happen because the discursive space is colonised by those who hold power and dictate the ways in which things must be said. For instance, a member of

---

3. That is particularly the case where education is seen as a private good to be purchased as an investment for an individual's future rather than as a basic commitment to the potential of young human beings and, indeed, all those who live in a society.
4. John Hughlings Jackson, or 'Remarks on the Evolution and Dissolution of the Nervous System', *British Journal of Psychiatry*, 33 (1887): 25–48.

an indigenous group might find access rights to health services are guaranteed, in principle. by legislation but still feel unable to access adequate and timely services because s/he feels awkward or wrong-footed when certain things need to be spoken about—such as a sense of being displaced or cut-off from sources of strength or affirmation in relation to the problem of youth depression and suicide indicators.

The ethical challenge posed by the need for partnership and negotiation in socio-political life is often illustrated by reflections on clinical life where the encounter requires mutual respect and openness of mind and the idea of intentional marginalisation or exploitation are not relevant. A person who is oppressed may find that the terms of a discourse are so slanted towards the discourse of oppression that they cannot say what they think needs to be said in the way that they would like to say it just as a patient may find that, with the best possible intentions, the health system and those who work in it make it hard to tell your story. For instance, the fact that a father of a family is constantly feeling worthless when he is not 'strutting his stuff' as a tough guy in the local drinking establishment and in the house may cause a great deal of harm. He may engender both fear and understanding in his children and they may feel unable to express the problem to anybody because of the shame they feel and their love and loyalty for their father. The story that they could tell in the contexts offering them help is unlikely to be understood in terms of the anger of the oppressed and the feeling of helplessness engendered by the socio-political nexus. The lack of any positive resolution of this problem hiding behind a wall of silence can then give rise to a meta-theory of human social being that is even more disempowering, as it subtends a discourse of individual fault and failure and the need for external rescue or intervention into the badness within the disadvantaged margins of society. The crusading intervention on behalf of internal suffering may be extremely violent and alienating and, in effect, make problems worse because the differences (of, for instance, differently abled people, ethnic minorities, and colonised groups) are not seen as treasures but as contributors to the problems (for instance of child abuse and neglect or teenage pregnancy). But 'badness' in such contexts is sometimes so intertwined with 'goodness' (or potential goodness) that the job of picking them apart can only be done with real sensitivity to the "inside" of things, as experienced by those concerned and communicated in terms not immediately accessible from without. If that is true, then attending to silences and the lack of voice, or a sensitivity to what is unsaid and puzzling, may be a guide to what needs caring attention.

In fact the need for empathic and imaginative listening is a constant theme of those impaired in their ability to communicate with us and to live an unassisted life. The narrative 'filling in' possible after attention to silences in a person's story may be particularly important in areas where we question ourselves *vis a vis* the 'differently-abled' members of society and their moral standing. The 'canary in the mine' is, of course, an instrumental fragile individual whose sole function is to prevent harm to significant others but the signal that the ailing canary gives is even more morally important when the canary itself is a precious fragility and should not be discounted as and ethical being enmeshed in discourses that produce our attitudes to ourselves.

The Human Group and its Maintenance—Our Form of Life

Aristotle, a naturalistic philosopher, examined what made for a good human life considering that phenomenon to be a version of a biological life as we find it in the world around us. The distinctive feature of human life is that it is predicted on the human intellect and our developed social or political functioning. That is the key to the fact we are 'promising primates'.[5] We engage with each other in terms of long term relationships based on a recognition that each of us is unique and has a unique place in a social context where lasting relationships and commitments bind us together. This characterisation is both natural and, in an Aristotelian sense, normative in that it explores not only the distinctive features of our adaptation but also what constitutes a good human life, the desiderata arising from a considered view of human life and excellence.

Aristotle argues that there is a certain way of living that intuitively strikes most people as good or as evincing well-being and that it has to do with what makes life as a human being go well in an analogous way to that in which an animal's life might go well. the over-riding context is the fact that we are beings who are born very immature and to thrive must be included in loving relationships where each of

---

5. P Wilson, *Man the Promising Primate*, (New Haven: Yale University Press, 1983).

us is nurtured in his or her being and gives expression to his or her individual gifts. In fact these very minimal requirements create some fairly robust constraints on what counts as a good life for creatures who live in social and communal groups and who exercise individual reason and creativity on the basis of the discursive resources created in those groups.

Aristotle moves from a consideration of animal and vegetative life to a consideration of distinctly human living which involves both reason and social relationships. The intellectual aspect of such a life includes the ability to reflect upon our actions and to modify them in the light of their impact on others and our complex relationships with those others. The social aspect of our being should allow us to consider those irreducibly social goods that are part of human well-being: love, friendship, loyalty, belonging, a sense of dignity and justice which informs the way we treat each other and so on. But we can ask whether such features of human life are sufficient to ground moral demands and duties or whether they merely define very relativistic, situational and even hedonistic reasons for and against certain actions. How do we ever get statements with the force of 'thou shalt' and 'thou shalt not' out of this somewhat flimsy network of considerations.

Going Neurocognitive with Hughlings Jackson.

John Hughlings Jackson used evolutionary theory to argue that the integration of diverse cognitive processes is the basis of higher mental functions and proceeds on the basis of 'propositionising' such that human beings use the 'service of words' internally and externally to formulate ways of acting in complex situations. Moral contexts require human beings to find a point of reflective equilibrium about a situation that matters (that is has emotional effects on) self and others.[6] Such a conceptualisation of moral reasoning implies that moral judgment, like meaningful speech, is 'a precise adaptation to new and

---

6. John Rawls' 'reflective equilibrium' is an exercise whereby we balance general principles of right action against the intuitive demands of a particular situation to arrive at a response to that situation that seems right (*A Theory of Justice* [Oxford: University Press, 1971]). Developing the ability to find reflective equilibrium depends on and results in a kind of phronesis or practical wisdom of the type Aristotle discusses in the *Nicomachean Ethics*.

special circumstances'[7] arising as we face the demands of living in the human life-world. Neither an impartial calculation of consequences nor an intuitive response based in emotion delivers an awareness of 'what in human social and personal life means something' sufficient to sustain the kind of moral reasoning we need in 'interesting times'. Thus a highly evolved and inclusive set of concerns goes into a well reasoned moral response and it depends on having information that captures the various aspects of a situation as they affect and may affect any human beings involved.

A wide receptivity for emotive aspects of situations and an informed social perception alert to the interpersonal complexities of life situations, particularly as they involve oneself, are therefore central to developed moral judgment and the integration of a heightened sense of human vulnerability and the discursive position of the vulnerable is particularly likely to broaden one's awareness of possible dangers to sensitive human interaction. To be alert to those aspects is not easy for people who are self-sufficient and well established in their life station and to achieve the flexibility of imagination and regard for others is important in the complex interplay of 'reservoirs of energy' and 'resisting positions' that mark human moral behaviour.[8] These come into being as we develop habits of reacting to and interacting with others and, at the highest level, incorporate the lives of others and what matters in those lives into the control we exercise on our own behaviour. This set of re-representations takes us above higher order combinations or patterns related to our own biological preferences and interests and entangles us with others in 'propositionising' about our actions and that is an order of cognitive integration indicative of a level of evolution not found elsewhere in the animal kingdom. What is more, when we seek actively to understand and accommodate the view of the most vulnerable, we open ourselves to a sensitive and nuanced awareness of the human life-world and its dangers.

---

7. John Hughlings Jackson, 'On Affectations of Speech from Disease of the Brain', *Brain* I.III (1879): 203–222.
8. John Hughlings Jackson, 'Remarks on the Evolution and Dissolution', *British Journal of Psychiatry*, 33 (1887): 32.

Moral Demands and the Human Form of Life

To understand this further we can investigate the thinking of a philosopher who regards moral demands as being absolute and thoroughly grounded in our shared life together. Wittgenstein remarks 'Ethics is the enquiry into what is valuable, or, into what is really important, or into . . . the meaning of life . . .what makes life worth living, or into the right way of living'. In response to the objection that someone does not want to behave any better than he does he remarks, "Well you ought to want to behave better."[9]. But how does he get to this absolute stance from his naturalistic and ethological starting point?

Wittgenstein locates all statements in forms of life where people communicate and share their lives by talking about what is around them ('That is a dog', 'That is my mother', 'Dad takes care of me', 'That is cruel', 'People need to eat and drink', 'Pain is not nice', and so on). The result is a network of practices that bind a group of human beings together by creating common expectations and patterns of interaction. Propositions reflect the general thought <that is how things are around here> and moral propositions are a subset that capture <how we do things around here> or <how one ought to behave around here>. In such a milieu of shared human activity articulated by language one negotiates a way of living. A human psyche is a product of participation within that setting and the prevailing norms of the group, converged upon by argument and agreement, form significant aspects of who one is as a person among others.

In effect, Wittgenstein answers the question about the reality of moral values in a way reminiscent of an 'old timey' (or 'down home') conversation about marriage.

'Jed, do you believe in marriage?'

'Believe in it, Hell, I seen it!'

Moral values are commitments and judgements that are basic to conducting oneself as a well functioning member of a human group who are living together in a way that enhances their mutual wellbeing.

---

9. L Wittgenstein, 'Lecture on Ethics', *Philosophical Review* 74 (1965): 3–26, 5.

One participates in this milieu, learns to see what is happening, and is changed by it into conformity with a kind of fellowship exemplified by the meta-ethical concepts of mortal sense and moral perception.

Moral Perception and Moral Sense

The idea that we directly or indirectly perceive states of affairs which ground factual beliefs is fundamental to empiricist philosophy and it implicitly involves a kind of imagination according to which we implicitly assimilate the current situation to others so as to abstract the feature being perceived (the colour red, the shape of a tree, the fury of a woman spurned, and so on). On this basis, empiricists often argue that moral facts must be 'queer' because they cannot be perceived in the same way as other facts because they involve values. However, virtue theorists, such as Aristotle, observe that we can directly pick up certain features of our shared human environment including features with implications for moral judgements such as 'he is a cruel man' or 'that was a very hurtful thing to do to him' or 'what a kind and thoughtful gesture'. Picking up such features depends, like many perceptual capacities, on skills resulting from a certain kind of training. Moral training sensitizes one to aspects of interpersonal situations which allow fine-grained and often subtle judgments about human distress, cruelty, concern, kindness, manipulation, oppression, and so on. Detecting such things is useful to creatures such as ourselves and there is every reason to believe that finely tuned neural networks such as those we possess might find them salient. What is more, once noted, the relevant facts would be expected to move us in certain ways.

Wittgenstein's later philosophy stresses the rules and techniques we learn in human forms of life and therefore welcomes this conception of perception and cognition. We can, in fact, find within it useful and interesting insights into certain kinds of mental disorder such as autism and psychopathy where interpersonal understanding is quite deficient in developmentally and morally relevant ways[10]. We can also usefully reflect on the availability of the perspective of the other to inform such an imaginative exercise. Through talk with others and the insights they express when we discuss situations, we often

---

10. G Gillett, *The Mind and its Discontents* (Oxford: University Press, second edition, 2009).

become alert to features of a situation that may have eluded us; 'You mean you didn't even see that, however good a face they were putting on it, there is something going very wrong with their marriage?' That particularly applies to those in a more vulnerable position: 'Did you notice how, whenever she went to say something, he always cut in with his version of events?'

Our perceptions and sensitivities can also be enriched and refined by the way that human situations are explored in literature and film. The detailed exploration of human reactions and responses and the vulnerability of certain human beings can be laid bare for us in great literature and can inform our moral judgments about life situations that we have never personally experienced. Jane Austen is a very polite but highly sensitising writer about nineteenth century Western society and its inequities. Franz Kafka often conveys the view of the oppressed, alienated and marginal in ways that otherwise we would not be aware of and *Wild Swans* brought to our attention the plight of ordinary human beings doing their best in the face of social reforms that often wore the trappings of what is right and good and just as a social program.[11]

The idea that we are creatures who form relationships with each other, care for each other, react to others in morally relevant ways and shape each other as participants in communities is fundamental to understanding ourselves as moral beings. It is ridiculous to argue that the realities that come into existence in that context are somehow less real than the sticks and stones that we find in the world in which 'we live and move and have our being'. We are equipped for relationships as one of our fundamental design features so that the absolute basis of morality, whether we correctly discern its implications or not, is in the quality of our relationships with each other and the value each of us puts on him or herself as a unique individual in the human universe of life stories. This conception of morality implies that there are truths about human needs and how we ought to treat them that are available to natural reason and instilled in us by the educative effect of ordinary experience.

---

11. Jung Chang, *Wild Swans: Three Daughters of China*, (London: Simon and Schuster, 1991).

Love and Life Stories.

Post-modernism foregrounds the multiplicity of stories and values that cluster around and in part constitute a human being who has traversed a unique path through our shared world and, in so doing, become an enigma, infinitely connected and yet utterly accessible and vulnerable.[12] An inherent instability, intertextuality, subjection to relations of power, and an essential partiality or incompleteness characterizes a post-modern way of doing ethics as distinct from more traditional and coherent systems of metaethics, related to secular Anglo-American philosophy or religious meta-narratives. That effacement of unambiguous principles and rules of engagement arises from the need for ethics to be attentive to human experience and particularly the perspectives of those whose narratives can be set aside or submerged in the stories we idolise and positions we valorize. Clearly there is a central place for marginalised narratives both in understanding of our worth and in the appreciation of our fragility as flesh and blood beings whose ills must be shared because the good of each is related to the good of all potentially if not actually.

The complexity of moral life is captured by Martha Nussbaum in her discussion of Rawls' 'reflective equilibrium' as it draws on one's intuitions, principles, and character.[13] The dialectic between self and situation played out in the dance of perceptions, reactions, responses, resolutions, and commitments are the nub of the moral story and so often made obvious in the life and death realities of clinical life that it is no wonder that Stephen Toulmin concluded that medicine had saved the life of moral philosophy.[14] As one watches the kaleidoscope of reactions passing across the face of a mother whose child is pronounced brain dead, a man in the prime of life who learns he has an incurable malignancy, or a young woman who realises that the operation she must have will mean that she is destined to be infertile, one cannot treat ethics as an abstract study of concepts informing practical reasoning or a dutiful following of certain commandments which stand somehow aloof from the ills that flesh is heir to. Ethics

---

12. E Levinas, (1996) *Basic Philosophical Writings*, edited by A Peperzak, S Critchley and R. Bernasconi (Bloomington: Indiana University Press, 1996).
13. M Nussbaum, *Love's Knowledge* (Oxford: University Press, 1990).
14. S Toulmin, 'How Medicine Saved the Life of Ethics', *Perspectives in Biology and Medicine*, 25/4 (1982): 736–50.

in general is for creatures who sweat, bleed, love, and die and who live life in the presence of uncertainty about who they are and what, if anything, is the point of it all. Ethical challenges make us confront these things armed with our vulnerabilities, needs, skills of living, and commitments to one another, and aware that there are a number of paths that any life could take constrained but not determined by the natural endowments of the traveller.

Attitudes and Emotive Dispositions.

Hume's claim that emotion is the heart of morality is used, by neuroscientists to claim that moral thinking combines emotional responses and problem-solving processes. We recognise the conflicting demands of tragic situations and the time we take to react correlates well with the cognitive activity (associated with more problem-solving parts of the brain) required to come to a decision because we are convinced that it is important to try and get it right even though there may only be a least-worst outcome. Notice that both immediate and more deliberated judgments involve both reason and a feeling for what is involved. The moral weight of an ethically demanding decision (based on compassion and a response to human suffering) is emotively registered and should guide, but not overwhelm or determine, our thinking in a mode of decision-making that incorporates, to a greater or less degree many other aspects of social and moral cognition.

Objective duties based on social roles, the requirements of law, and a reasoned appraisal of what duty requires are not the same as intuitive or emotive features of our moral life. A sense of duty may be compelling and demanding because I have been raised in such a way that certain options are not open to me—'Here I stand I can do no other!'—but I can and do reflect on those stances as part of my participation in the life of argument. The second nature inculcated in me by my upbringing, can sometimes compel (as in grammar and spelling—'He lied to her upon the bed' or 'shism' without a 'c' are both just wrong) as can an intuitive sense of logic or reason ('Babies are animals', and 'We eat animals' does not imply 'We eat babies'). These quasi-intuitive convictions are absolute but we have been trained into them and similar intuitive 'rightness' may accompany habits of observation and reflection in the moral life. I may also keep my promises as part of the way we do things around here and I may intuitively react if someone treats an indigenous person with disrespect on account of their indigeneity. I may feel discomfort when things are done in a certain way because, it is second nature to me notice the anomaly. The rational, ordered, calculating brain and those parts that intuitively inform our dealings with others are integrated in such moral reasoning and problem solving so that we act in accordance with sense and sensibility but not necessarily as a result of deliberation.

When Levinas challenges us to see what is before us—the faces, eyes, souls of other human beings each with his or her own life to live he draws out attention to a fundamental fact of our human life-world. Moral judgment, especially when it is challenging and personal, engages us with that ground of our being and draws on a wide range of information and many influences that must be integrated to produce coordinated perception and action. These include:

(i) primitive organismic patterns laid down during our phase of primary intersubjectivity and infant-mother exchanges;
(ii) the social cognition that allows us to recognise what others are doing and develop secondary intersubjectivity and a 'theory of mind';
(iii) an awareness of the negative effects we are having on others and a tendency to adjust our behaviour to that (lacking in psychopaths);[15]
(iv) a developed sensitivity to speech and conversation and the complex interpersonal and discursive knowledge that it enables;
(v) an alertness to those at the margins and, if we are appropriately attuned, an understanding of their alienation and its damaging effects.

These sources of knowledge about our world and their to the enactment of a narrative identity jointly show the truth of Hughlings Jackson's remark '*Le moi est une coordination*'.[16]

---

15. G Gillett, *The Mind and its Discontents*, especially chapter 9.
16. John Hughlings Jackson quotes this remark, by the French psychiatrists Ribot, with approval as a summation of his own view on the evolved state of integration

We intuitively see ourselves as moral beings and it is clear that our self-conception in that respect is not merely the hangover of a now outdated world view but a reflection of the way we deal with the challenges of being human? Cognitive neuroscience, treating us as evolved creatures with complex subjective lives reveals the extent to which we are formed by the many sources of information available to us in a lived context. That diverse information lays before us the lives of others and allows us to exercise moral judgment and empathy and not just calculate the advantages in any situation from a self-centered perspective. Moral being therefore integrates us into the human life-world and, as such, connects our lives to those with whom we share that world. In so far as those perspectives are enriched by the lives of others who are vulnerable to the slings and arrows of outrageous fortune, they offer us resources to understand our own moments of alienation and suffering.

The mirror world is the world created by discourse and it reflects many different images of self and others. For some the mirror is crack'd—the cultural resources they use to understand themselves as belonging to a particular human group with a distinctive history and sources of identity have been damaged or substantially destroyed (language survival is a good indicator). They therefore lack the means to see themselves clearly within the events defining human history (such as the move to cities, war, colonization, capitalism, and global warming). When a life or a body is broken as compared with the idealised images portrayed for us or constructed in our own minds the mirror also presents a crack'd image. The crack'd mirror and its images form a motif revealing the tensions of a post-colonial, post-industrial, post-enlightenment, post-modern world trying to adjust to the death of God and many traditional frameworks of meaning. But amidst all these the search for the moral ground of our being is a profound challenge that faces each of us and we cannot escape it as it links together diverse aspects of our function as creatures trying to construct a morality and system of justice adequate to the messiness of human life.

The moral life forces us to confront reality and not live a life built on slogans and illusions, it grounds us in practices, stories, icons, and

---

and coordination of neural function that makes any one of us a conscious and distinctive individual with our own internal checks and balances and sources of energy and inspiration.

myths that are the roots of our being and vital for our well-being. Colonization, injustice, displacement, injustice, urbanization, and the fragmentation of society combine to make us nomads 'in search of a soul' and nomads or gypsies, often find the structures of conventional, striated, society hugely distorting and constricting. Thus we come again to the canaries on the mind that is a human society with its many possible sources of misunderstanding and injustice.

An Evolutionary Basis for the Care and Value of the Fragile

The fragility of goodness matches that fragility of human life. We are creatures whose capacity to transcend material circumstances and use imagination and reflection to picture life in ways that may not ring true with our embodied existence as beings-in-the-world-with-others (Dasein-Mitsein).[17] It then emerges that the naturalistic axioms on which we can ground morality are as follows:

1. Human beings share a biological form or nature.
2. We are all members of an interactive community.
3. Different individuals have different perspectives on human situations.
4. Each perspective arises in a discourse that positions a subject in the human world and attaches value to the things that happen there.
5. Much is to be gained by sharing the knowledge arising from different perspectives.

These are all descriptive propositions (and therefore naturalistic) but an adaptive response to them (a response grounded in practical reason) generates moral or prescriptive theorems and corollaries which are, therefore, plausibly definitive (in an Aristotelian style) for human flourishing. The theorems fall into two groups, the first concerning an individual human being and his or her flourishing, and the second concerning our interactions with one another.

---

17. The phrase is from Heidegger and is meant to remind us that many of the separations between *mind and world* and *mind and body* and *self and other* are all abstractions from a more basic engagement and concern we have based on our being immersed in life and the world.

Theorems:

> a. A human being must belong somewhere or have a place to stand.
> b. A human being is a unique individual.

Corollaries:

> (i) We should appreciate the diverse knowledges that different individuals bring to any situation.
> (ii) We should attend to silences and discern why they are happening.
> (iii) We should be wary of moral 'truth'.
> (iv) We should give special attention to those who are experienced participants in a moral situation.
> (v) We should attend especially to those who are most fragile because they reveal to us points of vulnerability for critters like us.

Theorems

The first two foundational theorems ground all the corollaries and, because they arise from the general naturalistic axioms of human morality and therefore have fairly universal implications. The foundations are naturalistic in that they emerge from our conception of what a human life is and must be if the human being concerned is going to survive, grow, and develop into adulthood but taken together they evidently generate the substantive normative corollaries that follow them. There is an interesting circularity between the two basic theorems and the last corollary—(v)—because the beginning of our engaged moral life, for each of us, is a position of dependence and vulnerability where inclusion allows us to mature and develop in a way that has the potential to create in us a well-rounded set of evaluative and reactive attitudes in relation to others.

(a) *A place to stand*

Every human being belongs (even immaculate conception falls short of spontaneous origin), in that each of has emerged from some womb or other (usually as a result of the conjoining of tissue from two human beings—cloning entails that there might only be one immediate forbear for some of us). If, once created, the human being is not nurtured through both intra-uterine and early extra-uterine existence then that individual will not survive. Nurture consists of psychological support and care, so that survival is conjoined with well-being. During development a human being develops relationships of a type which create the need to belong or share with others in significant ways throughout life. These relationships and the shaping that they bring about are therefore formative in human well-being (or its opposite) and there are discoverable constraints on that process in terms of psychological health. There is therefore a range of relationships and types of involvement with others underpinning the psychological well-being of any human being. This fact is colourfully captured by the Maori phrase 'a place to stand' and the concept of the people of the land—tangata whenua (where whenua is used to denote both the placenta and the tribal land). We are slowly learning that a sense of one's roots is essential for the health and well-being of any person and that its absence is a powerful source of discontent. We are also aware that certain types of treatment of children will result in scars that distort their relationships to others throughout the rest of life. Belonging is, however, only one foundation for the human journey; the second is the room to develop as an individual.

(b) *Living one's own story*

The fact that each individual is unique (genetically and discursively) implies that each individual human being is an irreplaceable resource for us all and should be valued as such. Of course, overriding values may occur from time to time but placing value on the individual as an individual (acting with some independence from a platform of belonging) is plausibly the right way to go in the light of what kinds of critters we are.

Corollaries: Our relationships

The corollaries follow from the basic position and they put substantial value on things that many people cherish (especially those who have turned to post-modernism as a reaction to white middle class values). These valued things include moral responses as learning from open discourse with others, a spirit of humility, the sharing of cultural and moral perspectives, deriding the exploitation of others and the concentration of economic or political power in the hands of an elite, and so on. Some of these orientations arise directly from the fifth corollary—we should attend especially to those who are most fragile because they reveal to us points of vulnerability for critters like us. That is the basis on which we become aware of points of exploitation and injustice and the practices that we (perhaps inadvertently) support that tend to marginalise, create resentment, alienate, intensify vulnerability and the social pathology of the oppressed and so on. The voices of the most vulnerable, the least powerful convey an indication that there is something toxic in the human environment which puts in danger vital aspects of the moral life and which should not be allowed to influence law or public policy. It then requires a great deal of political and empathic wisdom about the human condition to see what we should do to avoid making such mistakes.

All these beliefs about what we ought to do and be emerge as rational entailments of who we are and what makes us human. What is more this set of beliefs and attitudes is particularly suited to social ethics, medical ethics or bioethics in which the power of the white middle class male establishment can prejudice who will prevail in any meeting of so-called equals in a given setting (the winners always tend to be either the doctors or the lawyers). Thus in the face of a claim that clinical ethics is bound to be hamstrung by diverse moral views 'It ain't necessarily so!' if we heed the moral voice of the 'canary in the mind' and do not merely treat the fragile and endangered among us as a minority to be appeased or an irritant to be accommodated. Their true role is not only to remind us of the diversity of human life and well-being but also to demand of us recognition and witness to the human beings whom we could all become if the contingencies of life conspire to harm us through the cruelty of nature or our own insensibility to the kind of world we are creating.

A Loss Of Faith:
Law, Justic And Legal Ethics[1]

Allan C Hutchinson

'Laws control the lesser man ... Right conduct controls the greater one'
Mark Twain

Distinguished Research Professor
Osgoode Hall Law School,
York University, Toronto

Lawyering is big business. But the substantial price of entrepreneurial success has been bought at the perceived cost of reduced social standing. Although criticism of lawyers is far from new, it seems to be particularly insistent and widespread today. Lawyers are not only portrayed as being skilled at the dubious arts of manipulation and double-dealing, but also as being moral hypocrites because they defend these practices in the brazen name of 'professional ethics'. Along with used car-dealers and tele-marketers, lawyers are now considered to be among the least trustworthy and least respected of professionals. The keen force of considered judgment is that many lawyers have failed to grasp the full ramifications of the crucial distinction between operating as a business and functioning as a profession. Lawyers have acted in ways that either ignore the public aspect of their professional status or, more cleverly, interpreted that public dimension to be consonant with the business interests of the profession. This is an ethical failure of considerable magnitude.

In such a climate, it is not surprising that there are increasingly urgent calls for a more ethical practice of law as well as a more compel-

---

[1]. W Bradley Wendel, *Lawyers and Fidelity to Law* (Princeton: Princeton University Press, 2011).

ling theoretical account of legal ethics. In short, the legal profession is being asked to put their ethical money where their legal mouths are. It is to Bradley Wendel's credit that he answered this call and entered the ethical fray with his *Lawyers and Fidelity to Law*.[2] It is an ambitious effort to 'bridge the gap between academic philosophy (moral, political, and legal) . . . and the circumstances of actual practicing lawyers' and to provide a justificatory account of legal ethics that is 'about political legitimacy, not justice or ordinary morality'.[3] However, his performance is exceeded by his ambition. Wendel has not so much offered a new approach to legal ethics as offered an apologia for extant professional practices. The fact that he has done so with jurisprudential sophistication and technical subtlety merely compounds the offence.

In this essay, I will strive to suggest a more promising and less constrained approach to developing a defensible theory and practice of legal ethics. The main thrust of my stance will be that, if the lawyers want to receive more professional respect for their work, they will have to earn it by reframing their ethical duties and taking them more seriously. This will not be done, as Wendel recommends, by offering better explanations and novel justifications for existing practices. Instead, it will require a genuine willingness to change what lawyers do and, as importantly, how lawyers think about what they do. After providing an account of Wendel's project and locating it within existing debates on legal professional responsibility, I will offer two series of challenges to his justificatory theory of legal ethics—the first is jurisprudential and will expose the theoretical footings and failings of his account; the second will be more practical and look to its troubling practical implications. Throughout, my critical focus will be upon how best to move forward the debate about the relationship between law, justice and legal ethics in a more satisfying direction.

Keeping the Faith

(a) The Challenge
Lawyering is not simply another business. While lawyers are in busi-

---

2. W Bradley Wendel, *Lawyers and Fidelity to Law* (Princeton: Princeton University Press, 2011).
3. Wendel, *Lawyers and Fidelity to Law,* 15, 2 (hereinafter refereed to by page number in parentheses in the text).

ness and entitled to maximise its profitable potential, they are members of a *legal profession*. As such, lawyers receive special privileges because they serve much broader public goals than their own private interests; lawyering has an indispensable public dimension that sets it aside from other businesses. In this context, 'good lawyers' are not simply those who reap substantial material benefits from their practice of law. While there is a disturbing tendency to equate the level of professional accomplishment with the extent of material reward, this measure is misleading. Many lawyers maintain the highest level of professional competence and achievement, but are relatively poorly paid for their services. Instead, successful or good lawyers are (or should be) better understood as those who maintain the highest standards of professional performance whether they are paid large or small sums for their efforts. To be a successful or good lawyer, therefore, demands a certain quality of ethical performance that in important ways serves the public interest.

The challenge, therefore, for lawyers both individually and collectively is to develop a mode of practice that can be justified in terms of this more public dimension of professional responsibility. This effort has centered upon developing a style and substance of professional conduct that negotiates the difficult ethical space between the pull of general moral considerations and the push of a specialized professional role—how can lawyers be good professionals as well as good citizens? The traditional response has been to construct a 'differentiated role': lawyers might be entitled or even required to do things that would otherwise be considered unethical in non-professional contexts. Clients are perceived to be autonomous in determining their own best interests and lawyers are expected to advance those interests with unconditional vigor, unquestioning loyalty, genuine candor, and marked partisanship. Portrayed as super-technocrats, lawyers serve the legal system best and fulfill its broader goals of justice when they neither judge the moral worthiness of their clients nor the justness of their causes.

The difficulty with such a traditional model is that it can often lead to lawyers acting as the pilloried caricatures of common perception. They massage rules, distinctions, meanings, and facts to serve their clients' purposes. Indeed, on extreme occasions, they might well be empowered to lie (that is, asserting false statements) and cheat (that is, advancing unreasonable and unverifiable claims and defenses) on behalf of their clients.[4] Under the traditional account of legal ethics, personal vices might well be tolerated or even celebrated as professional virtues. This is a far from edifying, let alone inspirational account of legal ethics and professional responsibility. It is against this backdrop that Bradley Wendel's *Lawyers and Fidelity to Law* makes its entry.

(b) A Faithful Intervention
Wendel's self-imposed task is less to design an entirely new model of ethical lawyering and more to offer a more compelling justification of existing practices. He is upfront in stating that that his aim 'is to provide moral and political arguments for a version of . . . the Standard Conception of legal ethics' (6).[5] By this, he means that he takes the governing principles of client partisanship, substantive neutrality, and non-accountability as the appropriate ethical indicators of good legal practice; lawyers act morally when they advance client interests without judging them and without responsibility for so proceeding provided that they do so by legal means. Wendel's hallmark contribution is to claim that, by offering a slight twist to the Standard Conception, it is possible to propose a much more cogent and complete justification of existing models and modes of legal professional conduct. It is a bold initiative.

Although the Standard Conception model recommends that an amoral or conscience-off stance be taken by lawyers in fulfilling their professional duties, Wendel devotes himself to defending this pro-

---

4. For a sophisticated account of this traditional role, see, for example, Sharon Dolovich, *Ethical Lawyering and the Possibility of Integrity*, 70, *Fordham Law Review* 1629 (2002) and Trevor Farrow, *Sustainable Professionalism*, 46, *Hall Law Journal* 51 (2009). The origins and justification of this image are very much tied in with the operation of the criminal trial process. Indeed, if there is any ethically compelling purchase for this model, it is to be found in the role of criminal defense counsel. See Monroe H Freedman, Lawyers' *Lawyers' Ethics in an Adversary System* (Indianapolis, Ind: Bobbs Merrill 1975), 9–24, and David Layton, 'The Criminal Defence Lawyer's Role', in *Dallas Law Journal*, 379 (2004).
5. Wendel's work is part of a recent revival in defending the Standard Conception of legal ethics. See, for example, Daniel Markovits, *A Modern Legal Ethics: Adversary Ethics in a Democratic Age* (Princeton, NJ: Princeton University Press, 2008), Tim Dare, *The Counsel of Rogues? : A Defence of the Standard Conception of the Lawyers Role* (Surrey: Ashgate, 2009).

vided that it is interpreted to mean that lawyers 'protect the legal *entitlements* of clients, not advance their interests'(6, emphasis in original). This entails lawyers accepting that their role is not to manipulate law to serve better their clients' interests, but to respect the law and to do what they can for their clients within this ethical horizon. In short, lawyers are to be vigorous partisans for their clients' interests as long as it is based on an underlying ethical duty 'to treat the law with respect, not merely as an inconvenient obstacle to be planned around' (3).Once understood in this way, Wendel maintains that this will be sufficient to give the lawyers' traditional modus operandi the imprimatur of ethical propriety: 'as long as the lawyer acts within the law, her actions may not be evaluated in ordinary moral terms' (29). Indeed, he goes so far as to insist that 'the lawyers' job is to push right up to the boundaries of the law' (82), but no further.

Having made this small, but important modification to the Standard Conception, Wendel moves to his primary task of putting forward a more convincing defense of such a take on legal ethics. His most distinctive move is to insist that most legal ethicists have been barking up the wrong justificatory tree. For him, rather than seeking futilely to square legal ethics with the demands of general moral norms, it is necessary to reference the arguments and sources of deeper political theory: 'ethical justification of lawyers is not case-by-case, but systemic and institutional in nature' (7) and 'legal ethics should be understood as part of the morality of communities' (41). Once seen in this light, the traditional account of a strongly-differentiated role between personal and professional ethical commitments is not only thought to be much more understandable, but also entirely defensible. The ethical warrant for legal professional conduct is to be located in political theory, not ethical theory. Wendel puts his faith in the ethical lawyer's commitment to be a loyal stalwart of the legal system.

Within a society that commits itself to the Rule of Law—'legality is fundamentally a political value' (11)—and its institutional imperatives,[6] Wendel asserts that individuals are entitled to rely on

---

6. Although Wendell does not deal with it directly, his account is very much based on the American legal system and the ethical approach of American lawyers. Nevertheless, it seems reasonable to assume that his prescriptions and justifications also have purchase in other societies (for example, Canada, United

the full range of legal rights and entitlements in their dealings with the government and each other. The law represents the best compromise of competing values in a pluralistic society. And, because law is a validated product of democratic procedures, there exists an obligation to respect, if not necessarily to obey the law: 'lawyers must treat law as a reason for action as such, not merely a possible downside to be taken into account' (49). Moreover, if law is worthy of respect, then lawyers who follow and show fidelity to law in their professional behavior should also be considered to act worthily. Wendel's justificatory account of legal ethics, therefore, draws upon a markedly positivist account of law's nature that builds on the work of both Herbert Hart and Joseph Raz in which law can be identified as a matter of fact through its social sources, not its political wisdom or moral value.[7] In this way, in going about their law-respecting business, 'the role of the lawyer is a morally respectable one' (10) even though it mandates lawyers not to look to general or ordinary moral considerations for guidance in their professional pursuits; professional ethics are politically related to, but not reducible to ordinary morality. So depicted, ethical lawyers can appeal to the legal system 'as an excuse for what would otherwise be deemed wrongful conduct' (26).

Wendel warns that, in fulfilling their vital political role, the legal profession should not put its own professional interests or their interpretation of the public interest ahead of the citizenry that it is intended to serve. Lawyers' commitment is to the legal system and 'calling upon lawyers to interpret the content of law with respect to the public interest has the effect of reintroducing the normative controversy that the law is meant to settle' (210). Within such a justificatory framework, it would be unjust and indefensible if lawyers did more or less than ensure that people are able to access and activate their legal rights. For Wendel, therefore, not only is there no need for lawyers to act in solidarity with their clients' stance, but there are also important

---

Kingdom, etc) that share similar traditions of law and lawyering. See Allan C Hutchinson, *Legal Ethics and Professional Responsibility,* second edition (Toronto, ON: Irwin Law, 2007).

7. In short, he goes with the 'softer' Hart on moral incorporation, but the 'harder' Raz on obligation and authority. See HLA Hart, *The Concept of Law,* second edition (Oxford: Oxford University Press, 1994) and J Raz, *The Authority of Law* (Oxford: Clarendon Press, 1979).

political reasons why lawyers should remain studiedly indifferent to their clients' causes and goals. By anchoring legal ethics in political morality rather than in common moral values, lawyers are expected to exhibit and embody 'fidelity to law' in their individual and collective actions. So, 'if a lawyer manipulates the law to obtain an unjust result, the proper basis for ethical criticism is failure to exhibit fidelity to law, not the resulting injustice' (9).

This is an original and provocative account of legal ethics. Prepared to follow through on the operational logic of this stance, Wendel concludes that 'lawyers can lawfully do no more, *and should do no less*, than their clients are legally entitled to do' (168, emphasis added). So forcefully put, it is a demanding and uncompromising ethics. He not only views legal constraints as the floor of lawyering (as almost all lawyers and ethicists do), but also makes them its ceiling as well; lawyers are not only permitted to do anything that is legal, but are politically required to do so at their clients' behest. Unhindered by situational or local moral dilemmas, Wendelian lawyers can and should go about their robust advocacy on behalf of any and all clients 'without any moral qualms'(86). Under his political account of legal ethics, it becomes the ethical duty of lawyers to 'subordinate' (155) or 'exclude' (157) ordinary moral concerns from their professional resources or consideration.

A Jurisprudential Response

The central problem with Wendel's offering is that, for all its erudition and elegance, it is not so much an account or justification of legal ethics, but a denial that lawyering is an ethical undertaking. There is no place for ethics in his political manifesto of professional lawyering. There is simply the institutional demand that lawyers make good faith efforts to interpret what the law is in any particular instance in a reasonable manner. This seems to be such a minimalist and open-ended injunction—'*be reasonable*'—as to allow lawyers do almost whatever they want in the name of responsible professional behavior and with the stamp of ethical approval. Consequently, Wendel's prescription for the ethical malaise of contemporary legal ethics not only kills the patient, but it seems intended to do so. Under his scheme of legal ethics, there is little to discuss or wrestle with when it comes to acting professionally. If this engagement is a mark of ethical conduct (as I will argue it is), then Wendel has nothing to tell us. For him, the dilemmas of legal ethics can best be handled by proceeding as if they did not exist.

In order to focus my critique and to delve a little deeper into Wendel's arguments, I will organise my comments around three particular issues—the mushy methodological foundations of his approach; the ethical vagueness of a 'good faith' constraint; and the interpretive difficulties in giving any bite to his proposals.

(a) methodological

As a preliminary philosophical matter, Wendel signals that he intends to validate his account of legal ethics by a general reliance on 'wide reflective equilibrium'.[8] Whether viewed as a mode of epistemic justification or as a more pragmatic device, the methodological resort to reflective equilibrium calls in aid a to-and-fro deliberative process: moral intuitions or practices and theoretical principles are sought to be brought into temporary balance through adjustment and modification. In the field of legal ethics, this means that Wendel strives to work the methodological space between 'theoretical considerations and the actual norms followed by conscientious lawyers in their professional lives' (15). Accordingly, he moves between his theoretical commitment to a political morality of 'fidelity to law' and the Standard Conception of ethical lawyering in order to strike upon a slightly revised account of legal ethics that best mediates the pushes of philosophical principle and the pulls of professional practice. The result is his neo-Standard Conception that is based on the central imperative to 'protect the legal *entitlements* of clients, not advance their interests' (6).

The obvious limitation with this way of proceeding is that extant practices and intuitions are given ethical weight in the justificatory method simply by virtue of their existence; there is no critical threshold to be crossed before they are taken seriously as valid or credible ethical resources.[9] In Wendel's account, therefore, the initial reliabil-

---

8. See John Rawls, *A Theory of Justice,* second edition(Harvard: Belknap Press, of Harvard University Press 1999) and T M Scanlon, 'Rawls on Justification', in *The Cambridge Companion to Rawls*, S Freeman edition (Cambridge: Cambridge University Press, 2002), 139–167.
9. See, for example, Norman Daniels, *Justice and Justification: Reflective Equi-*

ity or deservingness of existing professional practices and intuitions about what is ethical for lawyers is taken for granted—'the actual norms followed by conscientious lawyers in their professional lives' (15). As such, the present approach to legal ethics in the form of the Standard Conception is open to minor realignment or recalibration, but little more. But this seems to beg the very question that should be at the heart of the ethical inquiry into the professional practices of lawyers—are existing models and understandings of legal ethics, no matter how 'conscientious' lawyers consider themselves to be, worthy of moral standing? While the answer to that might be in the affirmative, this cannot be assumed without more. Wendel must offer some basic and independent defense of existing norms and demonstrate how they are not systematically skewed or perverse. Without more, he is engaged in a very narrow and circular exercise of defining 'conscientious' by reference to whatever most lawyers do. He assumes that which he claims to be justifying; it is a classic boot-strapping enterprise.

(b) ethical

At the dynamic heart of Wendel's recommendation is the claim that 'the fundamental ethical obligation of lawyers is fidelity to law' (178). As such, the primary and perhaps only constraint in play in assessing lawyers' conduct is whether they have complied with the foundational requirement to interpret in a reasonable and good faith manner what the clients' legal entitlements are. Drawing on his more general positivist account of why lawyers should respect law, he hangs his ethical hat on the claim that 'the value of legality makes it wrong to engage in excessively "creative and aggressive" interpretations of legal norms when advising clients or structuring transactions' (117). However, even this negligible constraint is relaxed in litigation. Wendel distinguishes between litigation and non-litigation work, such as transactional or drafting activity. He contends that there is greater leeway for idiosyncratic or dubious interpretations in litigation because a third party (that is, judge or adjudicator) is designated to take institutional responsibility for the law's ultimate and authoritative meaning (70–72).

---

librium in Theory and Practice (Cambridge: Cambridge University Press, 1996), 21–46.

For Wendell, therefore, the lawyer's range and style of conduct derives from their efforts to make sense of pertinent legal rules or principles in a conscientious way. Recognizing that the law is not entirely determinate and is open to varying interpretations, the requirement of good faith interpretation is less about legal rightness and more about political reasonableness. This is all well and good as a general and abstract constraint on lawyers' conduct, but it seems entirely unsuited to the massive task – justifying the whole edifice of legal ethics—that it is supposed to perform.

First, Wendel needs some reliable and reasonably fixed standard by which to define 'good faith'. Like all the usual sweeping terms of professional codes like 'integrity' or 'honorable', it defies easy or uncontroversial exposition. Grounding an ethics of lawyering in such a term is to put the entire operation on an undependable footing from the get-go.[10] The major responsibility of any workable account of ethical behavior is to supply some guidance or structure to debates about dealing with hard cases. Of course, it would be unfair and miss the point of ethical theory to expect Wendel to offer some formulaic advice that can be depended on to handle recalcitrant ethical dilemmas. But it is surely reasonable to ask for some better metewand of ethical conduct than that it is simply done conscientiously. Wendel's proposal seems even more baffling when it is understood that one of his main reasons for abandoning conventional ethical theory is that it offers too contested and indeterminate instruction on right and wrong: 'people are likely to disagree in good faith about how to specify an abstract ethical value as a concrete maxim of action' (90). It is far from clear why legal interpretation should fare any better. Indeed, even a nodding acquaintance with law and lawyers cautions against law acting as a bulwark of determinacy in a seething sea of ethical contestation.

Secondly, for many, the distinguishing feature of good lawyering is the ability to make 'creative' interpretations: it is more prized as an enviable talent than stigmatized as an ethical failing. Admittedly, Wendel refers to '*excessively* creative and aggressive interpretations of legal norms' (117, emphasis added). But the line between lawyers

---

10. For my own efforts to explore 'good faith' in the adjudicative context, see Allan C Hutchinson, *It's all in the Game: A Non-Foundationalist Account of Law and Adjudication* (Durham, NC: Duke University Press, 2000), 180–215.

being moderately and excessively creative in their interpretive efforts is very fine and murky. Considering how much work this good faith duty to interpret is intended to do in the Wendelian scheme of things, it seems an unpromising basis on which to build a whole account of legal ethics. Good faith is too vague a notion to resolve detailed and subtle issues of ethical performance. Moreover, what would it mean to enforce this requirement against lawyers who were perceived to be acting too unreasonably or unconscientiously?

Thirdly, there lingers within Wendel's justificatory account an assumption that law is something that stands outside the work and world of lawyering. Indeed, to act as a viable constraint on lawyers' conduct, law must be able to be depicted as a body of norms that stands as something that is sufficiently separate from lawyers. While there might be some modest defense of the idea that legislation is created and understood independently, it is much more difficult to sustain the claim that common law and constitutional doctrines are generated without the considerable input of lawyers. The fact is that a legal system has the laws that it has because of, not in spite of what lawyers do: the clients they represent, the causes they advocate, and the strategies they deploy all influence the law's content and substance. So appreciated, it becomes less reassuring to connect legal ethics' legitimacy to the establishment of legal entitlements when those entitlements are the function of the very conduct that they are supposed to regulate and channel. This seems a gaping lacuna in Wendel's positivist-inspired account.

An instructive and revealing discussion of the 'good faith' requirement takes places around the issue of frivolity in pleadings. In a provision that is typical of many jurisdictions, Rule 11(b), (2) of the U.S. Federal Rules of Civil Procedure obliges lawyers to certify that any legal claims made in their pleadings are, among other things, "warranted by existing law or by a nonfrivolous argument for extending, modifying, or reversing existing law or for establishing new law . . . after an inquiry reasonable under the circumstances."[11] While there is considerable agreement about the need to discipline lawyers who burden the courts and other litigants with unrealistic claims, it has

---

11. Until amended in 1993, 'nonfrivolous argument' used to read 'a good faith argument'. See 'Nemeroff v. Abelson', 620 F. 2d 339 (2d Cir 1980) and 'Kinee v. Abraham Lincoln Fed. Saving & Loan Assoc', 365 F. Supp. 975 (E.D.Pa. 1973).

been notoriously difficult to agree on what 'nonfrivolous' means. It has only been found where there is clear evidence that no reasonable attorney could have concluded that such a claim *might* be established and also that it was made for improper purposes; the individual lawyer's belief as to reasonableness of claim is key. As one civil proceduralist has noted, "today's frivolity may be tomorrow's law, and the law often grows by an organic process in which a concept is conceived, then derided as absurd (and clearly not the law), then recognized as theoretically tenable (though not the law), then accepted as the law."[12] Such an experience is hardly supportive of Wendel's willingness to place all his ethical eggs in the basket of 'good faith' argument. While there is a strong case to be made for including a good faith constraint in any series of ethical injunctions, it is wildly optimistic to make it the almost exclusive benchmark by which to control and discipline lawyers.

(c) *interpretive*
Wendel concedes that his whole justificatory enterprise 'stand[s] or fall[s] on the capacity of the law to yield moderately determinate meanings' (176). He is very alert to the claim that 'law may be so manipulable that an obligation of fidelity to law is inherently unworkable' (13). Nevertheless, he is equally adamant that there exists sufficient determinacy to underwrite his justificatory account of legal ethics. For him, there is a 'zone of reasonableness' (53). While 'people are likely to disagree in good faith about how to specify an abstract ethical value as a concrete maxim of action' (90), Wendell maintains that what lawyers know is law and so they should be expected to adhere to its imperatives, not morality's more diffuse injunctions. Legal interpretation is presented as a craft that contains its own standards of excellence and reasonableness. As he puts it, 'being an ethical lawyer means doing well at the craft of lawyering' (211).

Of course, the debate over law's indeterminacy is heated and the stuff of protracted jurisprudential disagreement. Those critical schol-

---

12. Risinger, 'Honesty in Pleading and Its Enforcement: Some 'Striking' Problems With Federal Rule of Civil Procedure', 11, 61 *Minnesota Law Review,* 1 at 57 (1976). For a more jurisprudence-oriented discussion, see Levinson, 'Frivolous Cases: Do Lawyers Really Know Anything At All?', *Osgoode Hall Law Journal,* 353 (1987): 24.

ars who resist claims about law's determinacy do not make the absurd claim that law has no meaning or that there are no areas of agreement about law's meaning.[13] While rules clearly exist, the precise meaning of those rules is always contingent and elusive in particular circumstances. No set of rules stands apart from interpretive attempts at its hermeneutical appropriation; there is no uncontentious interpretation that can claim to be the authoritative measure against which other interpretations can be contrasted. It is not that fields of law appear as indeterminate or determinate in general terms, but that even the most apparently settled areas of law are always vulnerable to being destabilised and thereby reconfigured with sufficient effort by particular jurists at particular times and with varying degrees of success. The law is not simply there in its object-like presence, but is always waiting to be apprehended and fixed by the active crafting of its judicial interpreters and legal artisans. As such, determinacy and indeterminacy are not pre-interpretive features of the law, but the resulting products of legal interpretation.[14] Law's meaning is always parenthetical and can never be grounded outside the contingent and continuing work of legal interpretation.

Although Wendel recognizes the importance of these jurisprudential matters to his 'fidelity to law' account of legal ethics, he does little more than make repetitive assertions of there existing a 'zone of reasonableness' (53). He gives little sustained attention to how that might actually be achieved in a robust and reliable way. He says that the threshold of interpretive plausibility is not so low as a 'laugh test', but might be met 'if a lawyer would be comfortable in making the argument to a judge for whom she clerked, a professor she respects, or a colleague who is known for her good sense and judgment' (58).

---

13. For my own extended account of legal interpretation as a playful performance in law's language-game, see Game, supra, note 8 and Hutchinson, *Evolution and the Common Law*. All legal interpretation depends on the fluid and dynamic interaction between interpreter and text in a shifting context of social conventions, institutional expectations, and normative values.

14. See, for example, Duncan Kennedy, 'Thoughts on Coherence, Social Values and National Tradition in Private Law', in *The Politics of A European Civil Code* 9, edited by Martijin Hesselink (Alphen aan den Rijn, Netherlands: Wolters and Kluwer 2006); Duncan Kennedy, 'A Left Phenomenological Alternative to the Hart/Kelsen Theory of Legal Interpretation', in *Legal Reasoning: Collected Essays*, edited by D Kennedy (Aurora, CO: The Davies Group, 2009), 154.

Taking his lead from the disputed ideas of Owen Fiss,[15] Wendel is satisfied to put his jurisprudential faith in the traditional resources and techniques of the legal community: 'if that reasoning passes muster, by the standards of the interpretive community, then the lawyer is justified in ethical terms' (207).

Pitched at such a level of generality, this seems a tempting and viable solution. But, as crafted (and crafty) lawyers know, legal interpretation takes place in more specific and concrete circumstances. Indeed, in two of the main illustrative examples that Wendel relies upon, his insistence that 'for any given area of law, there is a core area of agreement in interpretive judgments' (22) begins to look more than a little shaky. Insofar as agreement exits, it will be as much about the shared substantive values and commitments of lawyers as it will be about technical merits of the lawyers' interpretive craft.

Resorting to the traditional chestnut of 'no vehicles in the park', Wendel argues that, while there is a penumbral area of uncertainty, there is a core of agreement that some situations fall squarely within the rule. He contends that 'if the statute means anything, it means that you cannot drive a souped-up sports car through the park' (15). Yet, as most lawyers would agree, that conclusion can become much less obvious or incontestable in particular circumstances—what if there was a sports car exhibition being held in the park? What if the sports-car was being used as a makeshift ambulance? By positing these hypotheticals, I am not asserting that the rule is meaningless or that there are not instances of determinacy. I am simply arguing that there is no uncontroversial, fixed or plain meaning that can be referenced outside of any particular contingent context or act of interpretation.[16] And, without such an available core of meaning, Wendel's claims are in trouble as a foundation for legal ethics.

The same problem arises in the more telling and troubling situation of the Torture Memos. Wendel wants to condemn John Yoo's

---

15. Owen Fiss, 'Objectivity and Interpretation', 34 *Stanford Law Review*, 739 (1982): 34. For critical responses, see Stanley Fish, *Doing What Comes Naturally: Change, Rhetoric and the Practice of Theory in Literary and Legal Studies* (Durham, NC: Duke University Press, 1990), and Allan C Hutchinson, Dwelling on the Threshold: Critical Essays on Modern Legal Thought (Calgary and London: The Carswell Company and Sweet and Maxwell, 1988), 125–182.
16. For my own take on 'vehicles in the park', see Hutchinson, 'In The Park: A Jurisprudential Primer', 48 *Osgoode Hall Law Journal*, 337 (2010): 48.

advice as being an indefensible and argue that it does not pass muster as legal advice at all: 'waterboarding is the souped-up sport car of the prohibitions on torture' (15). He leaves no room for doubt that 'the objection . . . is not so much that it is bad moral advice; rather, it is that it is bad legal advice—the law simply does not permit what interrogators at Guantanamo Bay . . . have done to detainees' (181). Yet, as much as he may wish it so, his laudable moral sensibilities do not warrant that 'there really is not any disagreement, in good faith, about the meaning and application of [waterboarding as torture]' (182). The problem is that, as long as Yoo, the memo-writer, believed that he was acting good faith in arriving at a reading of the law which was requested by his presidential client, then Wendel's dismissal of the legal opinion is much less convincing. Indeed, as Yoo himself said in a subsequent hearing before a House panel, 'there is certainly room for disagreement among reasonable people, acting in good faith, on these questions, but I still believe we gave the best answers we could on the basis of the legal matters available to us'.[17]

For all his declamations (and most lawyers' desire to condemn Yoo as not only a moral scoundrel, but as a grossly incompetent lawyer as well), Wendel is simply unable to be as categorical as he would wish and needs to be in establishing the operational efficacy of his moral injunction to show 'fidelity to law'. This is symptomatic of the more general failing of his interpretive claims. Wendel has little to say to lawyers or anyone else in those circumstances where we most need advice–when lawyers disagree about what the law is. It is hardly a recommendation for his account of legal ethics that it only works when there is a widely shared or relatively unchallenged agreement on particular aspects of lawyerly conduct or legal interpretation. The real test of any proposed ethical stance is whether it offers any assistance or guidance in situations where there is professional disagreement or contestation. And when you add to that the difficulties of pinning down the constraining moral force of good faith interpretation, Wendel's reliance on 'fidelity to law' looks even more problematic.

---

17. *Washington Post*, Friday June 27 2008. See John Yoo, Crisis and Command: A History of Executive Power from George Washington to George W Bush (Kaplan Publishing, 2010. See also Dawn E. Johnsen, 'Faithfully Executing the Laws: Internal Legal Constraints on Executive Power', (2007) 54 *University of California Law Review*, 54 (2007), 1559 and Kathleen Clark, 'Ethical Issues Raised by the OLC Torture Memorandum', (2005) 1 *Journal of National Security Law & Policy*, 55 (2005): 458–463.

A More Practical Approach

(a) Towards an ethical account of 'Legal Ethics'
Ethics involves putting limits on the pursuit of self-interest whether individual or collective. While there might be some overlap in particular instances, this is more by coincidence than design. An ethics that reduces only to the facilitation of self-interest is really no ethics at all. Of course, an ethical code is not an exhaustive compendium of right answers and settled guidelines. While it often recommends bounds on acceptable conduct and distinguishes good from bad behavior, it will be as much a set of resources to think about and decide what to do. As such, the development of a sound ethical framework will be not be devoted to listing a detailed roster of formulaic answers. Instead, it will be more concerned with generating a series of arguments and considerations which any ethical decision-maker can consult and weigh in reaching a suitable course of action; it poses a series of orienting questions as much as offers authoritative answers. Accordingly, a good ethical system is one that blends a certain theoretical coherence with a genuine practical usefulness.

In developing such an ethical scheme, it is important to appreciate the different phases and components of ethical behavior. These can be helpfully identified in a three-fold format consisting of moral sensitivity, moral judgment, and moral conviction.[18] Each of these inter-connected stages needs to be appreciated by those who wish to understand and pursue an appropriate practice of ethical professional conduct:

- *Moral sensitivity* is the capacity to recognise that a situation has moral dimensions, that it presents a choice of possible responses, and that its resolution may have implications, large and small, for all parties involved, including oneself;

---

18. I have borrowed the work of the cognitive psychologist James Rest and given it certain twists to fit the legal and ethical context. See J Rest, 'Morality' in *Handbook of Child Psychology*, volume 4 edited by P Mussen (New York: John Wiley, 1983), 556–619; J Rest, *Moral Development: Advances in Research and Theory* (New York: Praeger Press, 1986); and M Bebeau, J Rest, and D Narvaez, 'Beyond The Promise: A Perspective For Research In Moral Education', *Educational Researcher* 28/4 (1999): 18–26..

- *Moral judgment* is an ethical assessment about what one ought to do and involves drawing upon a rich understanding of role-expectations, situational balance, likely consequences, and moral integrity in order to justify a particular line of action;
- *Moral conviction* includes the self-discipline and perseverance to implement the decision by giving priority to the decided-upon moral course of action over other values or goals (for example, career advancement, personal relationships, hedonistic pleasures, etc).

Developing these skills and values is a difficult challenge for most people in most situations. But it is doubly difficult for lawyers. Not only do lawyers have to cultivate these qualities and resources in their personal lives, but they also have to determine to what extent these might need to be set aside in their professional roles and replaced by a different set of ethical capabilities. However, if lawyers are to live up to their obligations to act as a morally-motivated and morally-directed group, they must nurture a mode of practice that is equal to that task. As with most other areas of moral behavior, lawyering needs to develop a sophisticated framework that enables individual practitioners to grasp and comprehend the subtlety and sweep of the moral imperatives that are imposed by virtue of their public and professional lives.

(b) Wendelian wobbles
The fact is that Wendel has very little to tell lawyers about what they might do or how they might think about what they might do when they are confronted with the familiar ethical dilemmas of professional legal practice. When the going gets tough, Wendel has nothing to say other than 'show fidelity to law'. He concedes that 'there is nothing wrong with having a moral dialogue with clients about whether to exercise the client's legal entitlements' (135). But, apart from the fact that it is unclear what the Wendelian lawyer would say qua lawyer in such a dialogue, such concessions are unhelpful if moral considerations are simply not part of the lawyer's discursive universe: 'lawyers, when they act in a professional capacity, should be concerned only with the legal justice of the clients' situation' (11). Two of Wendel's

examples point to the moral vacuity of his general account of legal ethics.

The first situation is straightforward. B(orrower) is in financial straits and loans $5000 by way of a promissory note from his wealthy neighbor, L(ender). L lets the note lapse. A number of years later, their financial situations are reversed and L feels obliged to seek the money back from B. For no apparent reason, B directs his lawyer to defend an action by L. The central question is whether B's lawyer should plead a solid limitation defense against the claim. Wendel argues that, whatever the moral failing of the client, the lawyer not only can, but also should plead the limitations defense on behalf of B. 'Regardless of any moral qualms the lawyer may have" (28), he maintains that "the ethics of lawyers acting in a professional capacity is different from the ethics of ordinary people' (29).

In this scenario, there is considerable disagreement about what the lawyers should do and why; it is a classic problem that tends to divide many lawyers and ethicists.[19] Wendel's only advice to the lawyer is to comply, dissuade the client from proceeding, or withdraw (126–28). But there is no discursive framework or set of resources that Wendel offers through which the lawyer might be able to determine what to do. He is unable to say much by way of ethical advice other than that withdrawal should be 'a last resort' (127). While there is no easy or obvious answer to this professional quandary (and it would be silly to expect one), the worth of any ethical account is its ability to inform debate and structure available arguments—is there a distinction between what one 'can' and 'should' do?; is B a one-off client or is there a long-standing relationship?; are there other local lawyers ready to take the case? and how devastating will such a defense be to L's life? Wendel's account has little to contribute to identifying, let alone addressing these and other pertinent questions. By reducing ethics to 'fidelity to law', he rejects its characterization and resolution as matters of professional concern.

The second example is *Spaulding v. Zimmerman*.[20] Z's lawyer obtains a medical report on S that shows that S has an immediately

---

19. See, for example, Stephen Pepper, 'Lawyers' Ethics in The Gap Between Law and Justice', *Texas Law Review* (1999): 189–90 and Thomas Shaffer, 'The Legal Ethics of Radical Individualism', *Texas Law Review* 65 (1987): 977–79 (1987).
20. 116 N.W. 2nd 704 (Minnesota, 1962).

life-threatening aneurism as a result of a car accident in which Z is at fault; S's own doctor has missed this in his medical examination. Although the report is confidential, Z's lawyer has a duty to hand over the medical report, if asked by S's lawyer: no such request is forthcoming. Can or should Z's lawyer voluntarily give the medical report to Z's lawyer? If he does not, Z will not be able to have the necessary life-saving surgery and might die. But, if he does, Z's damages claim against his client S will increase substantially. Almost all commentators, including Wendel (173), agree that Z's lawyers should have at least consulted with his client about whether to preserve confidentiality or disclose. But there is sharp debate over what Z's lawyer should have done if Z insisted on keeping it confidential.[21]

Wendel's response is revealing. Noting that this a 'hard case' (74) in that the parties' legal entitlements—confidentiality on one side and the right to the document on the other—are evenly balanced, he concludes that:

> For my own part, I find the possibility of non-disclosure intolerable for moral reasons, but if Zimmerman refuses to give informed consent to disclosure, the best course of action would be for his lawyer to disclose anyway and run the risk of professional discipline. A ... suspension ... would be a serious harm to Zimmerman's lawyer, but it is one that he may be morally obligated to incur in order to avoid harm to Spaulding (75).

This response is baffling; it runs contrary to the whole thrust of Wendel's approach to legal ethics. It may well be true and noble that he considers that the option of non-disclosure is personally 'intolerable' for him, but he is unforthcoming about those reasons. Moreover, this personal response is hardly the basis for a decision to withdraw as Z's lawyer, let alone a general piece of advice to other lawyers to follow suit. The main point of his account of legal ethics is supposed to be that the ethical duty of lawyers is to 'subordinate' (155) or 'exclude' (157) ordinary moral concerns from their professional lives and 'as

---

21. See, for example, Roger Cramton and Lori Knowles, 'Professional Secrecy and Its Exceptions: *Spaulding v Zimmerman* Revisited', 83 *Minnesota Law Review* 63 (1998): 83.

long as the lawyer acts within the law, her actions may not be evaluated in ordinary moral terms' (29). Therefore, it would seem to follow that Wendelian lawyers not only can, but should and perhaps must respect their client's legal entitlement not to disclose and can do so without 'moral qualms' (86); this is consistent with his stance on Borrower's instructions.

If that is the case, it is hard to see on what basis Wendel is placing his own personal moral commitments above his professional lawyering duty in advising others to withdraw as a matter of 'moral obligation'. Again, Wendel offers no explanation of why this would be the case or even how we might go about reaching or not reaching such a decision. His 'fidelity to law' approach is simply not up to the task of unpacking and confronting some of the compelling issues that might arise for the legal professional in search of ethical guidance—can or should Z's lawyer find an indirect way to tip off S's lawyer about his discovery rights?; how is the relative proportionality of the rights in play and the possible effects of exercising them to be considered?; what pressure can or should be put on Z by the lawyer to 'do the right thing'?; and how might the interests of non-parties (for example, S's family) be protected from the effects of any decision about what to do or not do?

(c) Clearing the ground
I have been hard on Wendel for his failure to offer an adequate legal ethics that is worthy of the name. My main bone of contention is not that I necessarily disagree with any particular course of action that he might recommend in particular situations, but that he offers lawyers no genuine ethical guidance about what counts as moral sensitivity, moral judgment, and moral conviction and how they might incorporate such qualities into the ethical hurly-burly of their daily professional lives. Telling other lawyers what you personally might do in any particular situation does not amount to a theory of legal ethics. That theoretical task would require laying out a more subtle and sophisticated set of arguments and reasons that could be accessed and utilised by lawyers in identifying and reaching solutions to intractable ethical challenges. This is no small or simple task, but it is one that must be undertaken.[22] However, as a preliminary matter, it

---

22. Important efforts at this task have already been made. See William Simon, *The*

is necessary to clear away some conceptual debris that presently hinders efforts to move forward.

First, the place to begin any reconstructive project is with the Standard Conception of ethical lawyering and its institutional privileging of client partisanship, substantive neutrality, and professional non-accountability. Rather than grant it a presumptive ethical authority and institutional appeal as Wendel does, it is necessary to subject it to a more searching critique. While it has obvious and cogent appeal in the criminal law context (29–31 and 192–93), there are no compelling or consistent reasons to extend this rationale to the non-criminal context; the institutional dynamics and moral considerations of criminal and non-criminal practice are very different. This does not mean that some components of the Standard Conception (for example, confidentiality, conflict of interests, etc) are not worth keeping, albeit in a possibly revised form. But there will little progress made if the Standard Conception is considered to be the default paradigm for defining and evaluating professional responsibility. A richer and more nuanced theory and practice of legal ethics will want to put topics, such as client selection, litigation strategy, negotiation tactics and the like, back on the agenda of debate and development.

Secondly, it is imperative that legal ethicists, like Wendel, abandon their attempts to annex traditional legal ethics to a positivist account of law. Even within the positivist canon, there is no justification for treating the law's morality or substantive justice as something that is outside the lawyers' frame of reference or legitimate concern.[23] Although positivists can be distinguished by their insistence that the domains of law and morality must be kept separate in the conceptual effort to fix and identify the necessary terms of law's nature and validity, they do recommend that there are many other ways in which law and morality can and should interact. Indeed, leading positivists

---

Practice of Justice: A Theory of Lawyers (Harvard University Press, 1998) and David Luban, *Legal Ethics and Human Dignity* (New York: Foundation Press, 2007).

23. There are, of course, less positivistic accounts of law that insist that morality is at the heart of the legal enterprise, including the jurisprudential identification of law' defining nature. The most prominent of these remains Lon Fuller's insistence that 'fidelity to law' entails an inescapable moral dimension. See Lon L Fuller, *The Morality of Law*, revised edition (Yale: Yale University Press, 1965) and, also, Roland Dworkin, *Law's Empire* (Harvard: Harvard University Press, 1986)

are at pains to explain how positivism does not demand that lawyers pay no attention to law's moral content or substantive worth; much of their work is devoted to addressing the moral failings of extant law.[24] Consequently, it does not follow at all that Wendel's commitment to a positivist understanding of law should or can lead to an account of professional ethics that eschews resort to the moral merit of law's rules and doctrines. To advocate for such a hands-off and agnostic stance, as Wendel does, is a perversion of positivism, not a defensible corollary of it.

Thirdly, if lawyers are to be properly treated as 'public actors' (13) as Wendel intimates, then it is essential that there is a more informed and fuller appreciation of what public goals and communal interests are being advanced by lawyers in their professional practice. Without more, there is no justification for why the public interest should be thought to be exhausted or fulfilled by lawyers' facilitation of private interests. It is the element of public-spiritedness that sets lawyers apart from other tradespersons and that warrants their considerable privileges and powers.[25] As self-regulating professionals, therefore, the moral obligations of lawyers extend beyond exclusive concern with furthering their clients' interests. Instead, they should be expected, not simply encouraged to include the public interest in any mapping of their ethical obligations and professional performance. The fact that what counts as the public interest will be contested is more appropriately treated as a warning, not a negation of its importance.

Accordingly, a revised theory of legal ethics will need to reclaim

---

24. John Gardner, 'Legal Positivism: 5½ Myths', *American Journal of Jurisprudence*, 46 (2000): 213. See, also, HLA Hart, 'Legal Positivism' in Encyclopedia of Philosophy, volume 4 (Macmillan, 1967), 418; Jules Coleman and Brian Leiter, 'Legal Positivism' in *A Companion to Philosophy of Law and Legal Theory*, edited by D Patterson (Oxford: Wiley-Blackwell,1996); Leslie Green, 'Legal Positivism' in Stanford Encyclopaedia of Philosophy, http://plato.stanford.edu/entries/legal-positivism/; M Kramer, *In Defence of Legal Positivism: Law Without Trimmings* (Oxford: Oxford University Press1999); and Andrei Marmor, 'Legal Positivism: Still Descriptive and Morally Neutral', *Oxford Journal of Legal Studies*, 26 (2006): 683

25. See R Pound, *The Lawyer from Antiquity to Modern Times: With Particular Reference to the Development of Bar Associations in the United States* (West Publishing Company, 1953); T Parsons, 'A Sociologist Looks at the Legal Profession' in T Parsons, *Essays in Sociological Theory* (New York: Alfred Knopf, 1958); and Deborah Rhode, 'The Professionalism Problem', 39 *W & M Law Review,* 39 (1998): 283.

and rethink the nature of this public-spiritedness that is supposed to animate professional practice if lawyers are to retain the privileges and independence they presently claim. The argument that there is a strongly-differentiated role morality that lawyers are to interpose between their personal and their professional lives can only be justified if it serves the public interest more than it does their own self-interest. In short, it is incumbent on the profession to ensure that the interests of justice are placed squarely and regularly at the forefront of professional concerns. As such, the primary justificatory challenge is to interrogate the dominant models of the ethical lawyer that informs the practicing lives of lawyers. In particular, it will be necessary to develop a more sophisticated vocabulary and fuller set of discursive resources which will be up to the task of negotiating better the difficult ethical terrain of professional lawyering—on whose behalf legal services should be deployed? And how should lawyers operate in the service of those clients and causes?[26]

Conclusion

Wendel's 'fidelity to law' model is less a theory of legal ethics than a jurisprudential account of why there is little need for one. On his justificatory account, legal ethics is a casualty of the adherence to an uncompromising (and wrong-headed) positivism that squeezes morality from both the nature of law and the nature of lawyering. Within Wendel's stripped-down account, lawyers' professional ethics require

---

26. An unlikely source of assistance might be found in 'ethics of warfare'. Military officers have available to them a much richer and more demanding ethical framework than their legal counterparts to construe and reflect upon the waging of their respective wars. As Michael Walzer concludes, 'for war is the hardest place: if comprehensive and consistent moral judgments are possible there, they are possible everywhere;' see M Walzer, *Just and Unjust Wars: A Moral Argument with Historical Illustrations*, third edition (New York: Basic Books, 2000) Accordingly, it might be helpful to think about legal ethics in a way that is more consistent with and informed by the 'just war' tradition of military ethics. In a system that is likely to remain committed to an adversarial system, such an exercise has considerable potential to cast a fresh light on lawyers' professional responsibility and suggest some fruitful ways to rethink the ways in which lawyers' ethical duties and conduct are conceived. In short, such a comparison might not only recommend new answers to old questions, but also stimulate a range of new questions for consideration. See Allan C Hutchinson, *Soldiering On: A Fresh Approach to Legal Ethics* (manuscript-in-progress).

that lawyers do little more than vigorously pursuing their clients' ends within the bounds of the law: the only ethical constraint in play is the inadequately thin and minimalist one of 'respecting the law'. Viewed through this proposed justificatory account of legal ethics, Wendel's conclusion that 'in the end, being an ethical lawyer means doing well at the craft of lawyering' (211) is a celebration of neither the ethical lawyer nor the craft of lawyering. There is much more to being an ethical lawyer than being adept at the craft of lawyering. What we do with those crafted skills and for whom—constructing torture racks or hospital beds?—is surely part of the ethical debate that lawyers must have if they are to deserve the label 'ethical'.

Vol 1/ 1 2013

The Genealogy of Space Ethics

Jacques Arnould
Ethics Adviser, CNES - Centre National d'études Spatiales, Paris

Introduction: Ethics, a Task for Space

The consequences of a technological conquest are never predictable, and the space conquest which began in the mid-twentieth century is no exception to this rule. The development of astronautics certainly fulfilled the dreams and ambitions of its founders – the military personnel and scholars who pooled their knowledge and intelligence, hopes and resources, in order to send machines and then humans away from Earth's gravity, to travel around Earth and then on to explore the Moon and other planets. States were able to affirm or strengthen their sovereignty, paving the way to whole new territories in astronomy. But the space conquest also revolutionised the life of humans, often in unforeseeable ways, to the point that our societies have become heavily reliant on the incessant orbiting of satellites overhead.[1]

At the same time, questions emerged and took form with regard to the advances made by science and their technical applications. While obvious in medical research, which concerns humans directly, the need for ethics was not as clear in astronautics. It was not until the end of the twentieth century that space institutions and actors saw the real need to define an ethical framework.[2] This initiative may have been inspired by the definition of ethics put forward by Michel Foucault: 'By attitude, I mean a method of relating to reality; a voluntary choice made by some; that is, a way of thinking and feeling, also

---

1. See Jacques Arnould, *Une brève histoire de l'espace*, Paris, Editions Jean-Claude Béhar, 2011.
2. See Jacques Arnould, *Icarus' Second Chance*, xxx, 2011.

a way of acting and behaving which, all together, marks a belonging and presents itself as a task, probably similar to that which the Greeks called an *ethos*."[3] Thinking and acting: in the minds of those developing it, space ethics is not for intellectuals alone, nor confined to their offices or committees. It is a matter for every engineer who takes his work and mission seriously. Thinking before acting and continuing to think after taking action, in order to draw the lessons needed to prepare for the future, this is the *creed* of the actors who have sought to apply the words of Montaigne to space: "Nothing is so fine and legitimate as well and duly to play the man."[4]

This is one of the lessons drawn from the first faltering steps in space ethics: far from being singular, or even extraterrestrial, space ethics is a profoundly human and earthly domain, not only because of its origins, but also because of its purpose. The conquest, exploration and exploitation of space are human enterprises, perhaps even humanist enterprises.

The Forbidden Dream

From the time humans appeared on Earth, they have always raised their eyes to the sky. How could it be otherwise? Why make an impassable chasm between the need for light of so many living beings, turning their gaze tirelessly to the sun-filled sky, the weaving paths of birds against the blue, the long howling of wolves at the full moon, and the first signs of our ancestors' fascination with the cosmos– painted on the walls of a cave or raised at the centre of an encampment? I refrain from saying that the conquest of space is inscribed in our genes, because I know what unfortunate associations can come with the aura of genetics. Yet I admit, and even defend the notion, that the space adventure stems from the deepest and oldest layers in the biological nature of humans. Layers which their conscience and imagination, intelligence and genius can and must cultivate so that they may become, "like [their] masters and possessors" (René Descartes) rather than their victims and slaves.

---

3. Michel Foucault, *"Qu'est-ce que les Lumières ?"* (1984) in *Dits et écrits. 1954-1988*, Volume IV: 1980-1988, Paris, Gallimard, 1994, p. 568.
4. Montaigne, *Essais*, III, 3, Paris, Presses Universitaires de France, 1978, p. 1110.

The term fascination, as used here, is associated with the double meaning of attraction and repulsion, desire and dread. From this semantic perspective, the void is fascinating, like the situations and experiences that allow humans to approach the edges of their condition, to brush against the confines of their knowledge of themselves. And so it was, and so it is even now, with the sky which was long inaccessible and even forbidden to Earth's inhabitants. This was not solely because of the weakness, inadequacy and debility of their technical capabilities; with the confidence and pride characteristic of their species, they were always sure that they would acquire the means, and master them, if only by imitating the flight of birds. The more serious question, with graver consequences, was: is the sky accessible to humans? Can they dream, aspire and imagine one day navigating the sky, or even inhabiting it? Are they not only capable of this feat, but worthy of it, or perhaps allowed to accomplish it? This remained to be seen. The Greeks and their thinkers had summed up this manner of thinking by calling the sky the *kosmos*, seeing in it a unique harmony which kept order among the moving and stationary celestial bodies, and maintained the regularity of their movements. What a contrast with the sordid teeming and ephemeral chaos seen on Earth! Thus, the sky and the superlunary world were attributed with perfection and inalterability, while Earth and the sublunary world were associated with imperfection and deterioration.

This bipolar reality recalls the dualist conception of the human being as body and soul, matter and spirit. Moreover, while the sky is off-limits to mortals, it opens its doors exceptionally to humans who have succeeded in shedding their most earthly and carnal shroud. Gregory the Great, in his *Dialogues*, describes what happened to Saint Benedict of Norcia, the father of Western monasticism: "Benedict was at the window, praying to the almighty Lord. Suddenly, in the heart of the night, he saw a ray of light from above push back the darkness of night. The splendour of the light was even brighter than the light of day, which shone between the times of darkness. After contemplating this sight, something very marvellous happened, as he told it: as if lifted upon a single ray of sunlight, the entire world was brought before his eyes." Gregory goes on to explain, "For the soul who beholds the Creator, all of creation is small. Even if it has seen only a tiny part of the Creator's light, everything created becomes small to it.

In the clarity of internal contemplation, the soul increases in size; in God, it expands to become superior to the world." Thus, the ecstatic experience of Benedict and his mystical colleagues is not without a sentiment of superiority and power. In this view, wouldn't the sky be forbidden for the same reasons as the fruit of the tree of knowledge of good and evil, planted by God in the Garden of Eden? Humans who took possession of it would become like gods, and could even claim to replace them. When the first "heavier than air" devices were being sent into space, Clément Ader echoed this notion from antiquity, writing, 'He who is master of the sky will be master of the world'. This statement is probably one of the oldest, deepest and most important roots behind space ethics.

As both a founded and founding notion, the forbidden nature of the sky had a major influence on the religions, beliefs, philosophies and theologies in most eras and areas of the world. Before the Copernican revolution, before the West entered into the modern era and astronomic sciences shattered the crystal balls which had constituted and protected the cosmos thus far, the sky could easily represent a place for paradise, a mirror for utopias, and a sanctuary for dreams of perfection and innocence. It was a genealogical territory with earthly morals, to which it was itself exempt. Until April 1610, when reading Galileo's *The Starry Messenger* revealed to Johannes Kepler that the era of sky navigation had arrived, and that humanity could one day escape its earthly prison, its "little dungeon" (Blaise Pascal). But what ethics would humanity apply to this new freedom?

The Sky at Our Feet

In the preface to *The Breasts of Tiresias (Les Mamelles de Tirésias)*, Guillaume Apollinaire wrote, 'When Man wanted to imitate walking he created the wheel which does not resemble a leg. He did something surrealist without even knowing it'.[5] In the same way, several millennia later, in order to imitate the flight of birds, man would have to observe windmills and invent the propeller. Propulsion in the air would require more effort, even more ingenuity, and, to use the poet's expression, a surrealist approach, since in each case what is

---

5. Cited in Jean Brun, *Les conquêtes de l'homme et la séparation ontologique*, Paris, Presses Universitaires de France, 1961, p. 85.

required is parting from the obvious reality, the accepted logic, and even the usual ethics and aesthetics. One should probably not try to further associate the space enterprise with André Breton's work and his *Surrealist Manifesto*, but this comparison at least offers an interpretation of Hannah Arendt's assertion in *The Human Condition* that the launch of the Sputnik was an event "second in importance to no other, not even the splitting of the atom", claiming that this confirms the prophecy engraved on the stele of the Russian scholar Konstantin Tsiolkovsky: 'Mankind will not remain bound to the earth forever'. Indeed, a half-century earlier, as he was laying the foundations for modern astronautics, Tsiolkovsky had written: 'Earth is the cradle of Humanity; but no one can stay in the cradle forever'.[6] At the end of the 1950s, the pressing question was no longer whether the sky was accessible to humans, but rather what would humans become once they had crossed over the once sacred threshold into space? All of the hopes usually associated with the discovery, conquest and exploitation of a new world were once again becoming possible. The enthusiasm which followed the success of first space programmes during the 1960s sparked and triggered imaginations, not only in the field of artistic creation where works of science fiction abounded, but also in the sciences and technology, sociology and economics. For a brief time, perhaps, space represented another upheaval similar to that which, for the Europe of the Renaissance, came with the discovery of a new world – with its riches, its dangers, and finally its inhabitants. But, symbolically, the celestial window closed again when the last Apollo mission returned to Earth. Indeed, a frontier had been moved, and the earthly sphere had been widened, but the humans of the twentieth century had not had the bewildering experience which Western civilisation had at the end of the fifteenth century: they had not met an *alter ego*.

Although humanity was perhaps not as deeply shaken as Hannah Arendt may have thought or hoped after Sputnik's first flight, space would never be the same. It was no longer a forbidden territory, or a place which was technically out of reach. Space became a vast project site, an endless field for new human activities; it is what humans do there and what they make of it. Its limits are no longer just those imposed by philosophical reasoning and religious ideologies, but

---

6. In a letter sent to the engineer Boris Vorobiev on 12 August 1911.

also those imposed by scientific theories and instruments. The orbits criss-crossing across space are no longer just stars, planets, meteors and other aeroliths; now there are also satellites, the celestial and artificial companions which have become so essential to our daily lives. Space is now inseparably, all at once, a geometric and symbolic, scientific and technical, political and cultural object. Its definition, borders and horizons are those set out and imposed by our knowledge and our powers, our ignorance and our fears, our desires and dreams. Never before has space been so human.

Through their own ideological, legal and moral resources, humans have learned to think and act in space, according to Michel Foucault's definition of ethics. Above all, they have learned to manage a new power. In order to reach space and become a 'space power', a State needs to acquire certain abilities, and succeeding in this also increases its power and sovereignty. History shows that, in the conquest of space by the Americans and Soviets during the Cold War, the world leaders at the time were concerned with achieving a balance of power in space-related abilities, similar to that defended by deterrence theory. Of course the race to the Moon was won by the United States and probably accelerated the fall of the Soviet Union, but the nations were also able to agree not to reproduce the same national divisions in space (once technologically conquered) as there were on Earth. In this spirit, space was declared the common heritage of mankind, and the 'launching State' principle was developed.

The first article of the Outer Space Treaty of 1967 states that 'Outer space, including the moon and other celestial bodies, shall be free for exploration and use by all States without discrimination of any kind, on a basis of equality and in accordance with international law, and there shall be free access to all areas of celestial bodies'. Basically, this means that space is not a no-man's-land that could be occupied and exploited by the first to arrive, or by any subsequent parties. The Treaty defines space as being international in character and unable to be claimed or appropriated by any State. It must be considered as a public domain where everyone must ensure order, peace and equality between States. Making this declaration in the context of the mid-1960s was no trivial matter: with the United States and the Soviet Union involved in a fierce battle to be the first on the Moon, while also developing space abilities which would serve their armed forces, what this treaty proposed was to protect space from any national claims or military impulses, for space to belong to all of mankind. It makes a generous, prophetic and even utopian statement. It had the great merit of being adopted, supported and confirmed by States, of a varying number according to the texts proposed for their signature. The Outer Space Treaty was ratified by ninety-seven States and signed by twenty-seven others. The Moon Agreement was only ratified by twelve States and signed by four others.

The legal notion underlying the first article of the 1967 Treaty is that of common heritage. It describes what is stated to belong to everyone and must consequently be used for the common good, with everyone's share (for example, of resources) being guaranteed. The 1960s gave rise to the concept of the common heritage of mankind against a backdrop of decolonisation, the bipolarisation of international relations and the emergence of new North-South relations. It is also linked to the notion of "new international economic order" claimed at the same time by newly decolonised States, based on equity, interdependence, sovereign equality and interstate cooperation. Based on the proposal by the Maltese ambassador Arvid Pardo in 1967, the international Montego Bay Convention signed in December 1982 used the same common heritage principle, applying it to the seabed. It this case, the aim was to protect polymetallic nodules from any commercial exploitation, whereas the surface waters, or "high seas", found in international zones are treated as common property (in Latin legal jargon: *res communis*). They do not belong to anyone, and therefore can be accessed, used and exploited by all, possibly in accordance with certain restrictions or regulations. In other words, no State can claim sovereignty over these territories, and no national law applies to them, although the national intervention systems and fishing quotas are stipulated in international agreements. The continent of Antarctica is another example of common heritage of mankind.

So what about declaring space to be the common heritage of mankind? Morose or simply realistic observers would call this approach to space law utopian. After all, what will it be worth when there are major benefits to be gained from exploiting the Moon or asteroids? Earth's orbits, as common heritage, are already the subject of fierce negotiations for the placement of satellites, which generate profits.

The same fate probably awaits asteroids and planets which may contain rare minerals. I cannot deny this, but nevertheless, I am convinced that there is a unique aspect with space: that a framework and horizon have been established for the boldest and most far-off space ambitions (exploring, conquering and exploiting celestial bodies) along with the most immediate space services (transmitting information, observing events on Earth and human acts).

The responsibility of States in terms of space activities constitutes another significant aspect of space law, and space ethics. The sixth article of the 1967 Treaty states that: 'States Parties to the Treaty shall bear international responsibility for national activities in outer space . . . whether such activities are carried on by governmental agencies or by non-governmental entities . . .' In other words (and this is what makes space law so unique), all 'national' space activities are assimilated to activities of the States, whether carried out by their citizens or by foreigners in their country, by their nationals from the territories of other States or even from international zones. By virtue of Articles VII and VIII of the same Treaty, the responsibility of States Parties shall be understood according to two meanings: that of the control of the actual activities (*responsibility*) and that of financial compensation in the event of damage caused by these activities (*liability*).

The 1972 Liability Convention specifies the scope of application of this specific rule for the compensation of damage caused by a space object on the ground, in air space and in outer space, based on the notion of launching State. The first Article of this Convention defines this notion as follows: 'the term "launching State" means: a State which launches or procures the launching of a space object; a State from whose territory or facility a space object is launched'. In other words, this key notion of space law is defined based on four alternative criteria: the launching State, the State which procures the launching, the State from whose facility a space object is launched and the State from whose territory a space object is launched. In this way, for a single object launched into outer space, several countries may be recognised as 'launching States' and therefore be held jointly responsible for damage which may be caused by this object: 'a launching State has absolute liability for damage caused by its space object to the surface of the Earth or an aircraft in flight.' This liability has no statute of limitations, which poses a legal problem in itself, since launched objects can stay in orbit for centuries. During this period, the space objects may change ownership and, consequently, launching State, or a new launching State may become involved. They may also be moved repeatedly without the launching State(s) being informed, despite the fact that the latter remain legally liable. Launching States may also have to negotiate agreements to share the cost of damages. The victim can turn to the most solvable launching State in order to demand full compensation, in which case the latter can seek damages from the other launching States.

The notion of fault which is commonly used on Earth is more difficult to apply where space activities are concerned, since it makes explicit reference to a regulation which, in most cases, is inexistent or exists under different forms and titles making it difficult to apply. This is, in particular, the case of space debris in circumterrestrial space which has led space agencies to draw up several types of recommendations: the *Mitigation Guidelines* of the Inter Agency Space Debris Coordination Committee (IADC), the NASA standard and the European code of conduct. The way in which these texts define 'good behaviour' in space leads to several different and sometimes even opposing points of view.

The notion of fault also raises the question of evidence. How is it possible to gather evidence when the activities in question take place hundreds and thousands of kilometres from the Earth's surface, in zones that are difficult to access? Let us return to the example of space debris. The most readily available information about objects moving around in space is obtained via American space surveillance systems (see below). NASA regularly publishes and circulates a catalogue of objects moving around our planet. This document is of course declassified and does not go into full detail: it does not mention objects considered as sensitive by the United States. How credible is this information when attempting to investigate an incident to determine fault and liability? One-off or partial observations conducted by other nations have allowed the errors, mix-ups and even omissions of the American services to be highlighted whether these were unintentional (the identification of small and far-off objects is difficult) or deliberate. How can we therefore hope to provide tangible, solid evidence in the event of a dispute?

Finally comes the question of the implementation, monitoring and control of this law. We cannot simply define regulations concerning the use of space. We must be able to check compliance with these regulations by the different actors and operators and to set up independent means of observation. Then, if a breach is duly observed, for example, a violation of the principle of the use of space for peaceful purposes, a sanction would need to be applied. However, is it possible to establish such a system of space policing at an international level? More realistically, it is now recommended to ensure national application of the rules defined at the international level: each State is asked to establish national legislation in accordance with international space law. There is a real risk that we could find ourselves in the same situation as with the law of the sea, where the practice of flags of convenience exists. A State could in effect choose not to impose the application of international measures on its inhabitants and the companies on its soil, thereby encouraging the implantation on its territory of operators more concerned with cutting costs than ensuring the common good. For the time being, the main space States have signed and do implement the UN treaties. However, the risk of flags of convenience turning up in space cannot be ruled out.

Clean, peaceful and responsible – the dream for space today. This vision of space is like a twin brother to that of our ancestors, the one they called *kosmos*. What if humans wanted to conquer the sky in order to make it the most beautiful place on Earth? Especially when engineers, political scientists and entrepreneurs turn their imaginations to creating plans for the future occupation of space… In an article on space colonisation published in 1974, Gerard O'Neill confidently stated: 'It is orthodox to believe that Earth is the only practical habitat for Man, and that the human race is close to its ultimate size limits. But I believe we have now reached the point where we can if we so choose, build new habitats far more comfortable, productive and attractive than is most of Earth'.[7] The Princeton physicist also imagined creating a new Garden of Eden, in immense cylinders 1500 metres long and 300 metres in diameter, large enough to house ten thousand people. In these island habitats, he adds 'there will be insects, such as butterflies, for the birds to eat. But there need not be mosquitoes, cockroaches or rats'.[8]

---

7. See Gerard O'Neill, "The Colonization of Space", *Physic Today*, 27(9), 1994, p. 32–40.
8. Gerard O'Neill, *Les Villes de l'espace. Vers le peuplement, l'industrialisation et la*

This is a very human tendency, to want not only to take over previously unknown worlds, to which our observations and explorations have opened the doors, and not only to claim their riches and resources, sometimes even depleting them completely, but also to transform them according to our desires, dreams and ideologies. This is what has been done on Earth, and what will one day be done in space (according to O'Neill and other visionaries), as in other territories and dimensions, such as life or the nanosphere. And with this vision came a plethora of promises of the best of worlds and the best of humanities, perhaps even transhumanity.

Earth for the Ultimate Frontier?

Where do we come from? Where are we going? Humankind does not seem to have gained an ounce of response to these age-old questions, even since turning its telescopes to the sky and its microscopes onto the intimate secrets of life. And those who travel the skies in their spacecraft are still shared between the nomad's fervour for new horizons, and the sedentary individual's attachment to home. These are two very different dynamics for managing time and space, territory and history, available resources and their consumption. But humanity can no longer resort to a nomadic lifestyle to ensure its future, or even its survival. As astronauts and images from space attest, unequivocally: we only have one Earth, and there is no point in dreaming of finding or obtaining another one, at least not within a reasonable lapse of time.

In this sense, the space enterprise has changed nothing with regard to the German philosopher Edmund Husserl's observation in a 1934 study entitled *Earth, the original ark, does not move*: 'Movement takes place on Earth, directly against it, starting from Earth and moving away from it. The Earth itself, in its original form of representation, does not move, nor is it at rest. It is first and foremost with respect to Earth that movement and rest find their meaning.'[9] Husserl is not necessarily challenging Copernican revolution as such, but is making a statement

---

production d'énergie dans l'espace, Paris, Robert Laffont (Les visages de l'avenir), 1978p. 242. Also see Agnès Ricroch & Jacques Arnould, "Les jardins de l'espace", *Etudes*, 4004 (April 2004), p. 489-498.

9. Edmund Husserl, *Earth does not move*, Paris, Editions de Minuit, 1989, p. 12.

against too hasty a divorce between the sciences (here, astronomic science) and common sense. Husserl continues: 'All animals, all human beings, all beings in general only have a sense of being based on my constitutive genesis and that has a terrestrial precedence.'[10] In these words there is no anthropocentric pretension, no exaggerated pride on the part of Husserl and to the benefit of man, but only an observation based on the experience of reality and the correct understanding of phenomena: man remains at the centre of his own experience of the world, whether at rest or in motion. Jean-Jacques Salomon adopts the following opinion: 'Our human horizon remains on Earth, despite scientific and technological progress.'[11] While space has not been fully integrated into human ethics, the progress in astronautics demands that ethics at least be given a planetary dimension.

In the early 1960s, Marshall McLuhan did not in the least adhere to the notion of entrapment or imprisonment. Instead, he became an advocate of the global village, or planetary village, concept. In 1962, he wrote: 'Information comes to us from all over at accelerated speed, at electronic speed. It is as if we are part of a little global village.' Fifty years later, the phenomenon that McLuhan described only continues to speed up and grow, to the point that we now suffer from too much information, and our abilities to pay attention are overloaded. Dominique Wolton wonders whether the global village, having become a technical reality, is an actual social and cultural reality, or whether "the interests of the communication industries" have not been confused with the 'philosophical and socio-historic reality of the users of these communication techniques.'[12] In any case, thanks to space technology, the innumerable networks which criss-cross, surround and encircle the Earth make it possible (without venturing down the steep, harsh paths of mysticism) to live something similar to Saint Benedict's experience: that is, holding the world under a single ray of sun, on a computer screen or mobile phone, and possessing it with the click of a mouse or the pressing of a key. Quite the opposite of distancing us from our planet, space has actually brought it closer to us. It delivers Earth right to our feet.

---

10. *Ibid.* 27.
11. Cited in Jacques Arnould, *La seconde chance d'Icare*, Paris, Cerf, 2001, p. 216.
12. Dominique Wolton, *Internet et après ? Une théorie critique des nouveaux médias*, Paris, Flammarion, 1999, p. 130.

Among the most famous photographs in the history of this technology are two views of Earth, *Earthrise* (December 1968) and *The Whole Earth* (December 1972), taken by the crew of Apollo 8 and Apollo 17 while on their way to or orbiting the Moon. Should credit also be given to Alfred Sauvy, who, thirty years after the exploits of Sputnik and Youri Gagarine, said, 'The contemporary environmental movement began with walking on the moon'?[13] It is surely more accurate to see a certain concomitance, rather than causality, between the first *Apollo* missions around and then on the Moon, and the emergence and growth of environmental concern. Rachel Carson's book, *Silent Spring*, which symbolically marks the beginning of ecology, was published in 1962, and the first world summit on the environment took place in Stockholm in 1972. Concomitance, because the views of Earth brought back by the Apollo astronauts did not turn everyone on Earth into militant ecologists. The American astronaut Jeffrey Hoffman, who saw Earth from its orbit on five different space shuttle missions, expresses this clearly: 'It would be naive to think that all we have to do is take pictures of Earth from space, and that by promoting environmental awareness this way, all of the problems will be resolved.'[14] Space on its own will never resolve any of the problems on Earth. It will, however, be a wake-up call for the inhabitants of Earth, and be instrumental in calling them to action. Space does not need its own special moral code; rather, it calls us to explore new dimensions of earthly and human ethics, and to place greater emphasis on certain aspects. In my opinion, the value and virtue of fraternity is one such aspect.

'Yes, we are calling all European governments, in the Europe of twelve members, to consider every possible means, including the use of force in order to stop the war. Tomorrow, they will not be able to say that they did not know; they will not be able to say that they could not.' With these words on 21 November 1992, the French journalist Jacques Julliard concluded a silent demonstration against President Milosevic's ethnic cleansing policy.[15] The same phrase was used

---

13. Alfred Sauvy, preface to *L'Etat de la planète*, Paris, Editions Economica, 1990.
14. Jeffrey A. Hoffman, "A personal account of spaceflight", in Jean Schneider & Monique Léger-Orine (éd.), *Frontières et conquête spatiale. La philosophie à l'épreuve*, Dordrecht/Boston/London, Kluwer Academic Publishers, 1988, p. 203.
15. Based on Jacques Julliard, "Nous ne pourrons pas dire que nous ne savions pas",

on other occasions, for example, by President Jacques Chirac at the World Summit on Sustainable Development, in Johannesburg in September 2002, and in the mid-1980, by a non-governmental organization to alert the French public to the humanitarian catastrophe in the Sahel region of Africa. This expression sums up what I would refer to as the principle of vigilance, the tension between knowing, being able to act and taking action, between what has already been done and what is still possible. The eye which followed Victor Hugo's version of Cain to the tomb, in other words, the eye of his conscience, is now equipped with technological means which are literally exorbitant: we can no longer say that we, each of us individually, do not know what is happening on Earth.

Nearly fifty years ago, Jürgen Habermas already questioned his contemporaries: 'How can the ability to technically possess things be reincorporated into the consensus between citizens involved in different actions and negotiations?'[16] One possible answer to this question is fraternity. 'Am I my brother's keeper?' asks Cain of God. The answer is clearly 'no'. His brother does not need to be kept and it is not Cain's right or duty, nor does he have the power or authority, to control his brother's behaviour, or to hinder his freedom to act. But was that really God's reproach? Wasn't it rather that he had forgotten the bond of fraternity that tied him to Abel, and at the same time his bond with the Earth?

Conclusion

The astronomer Arthur Eddington made the following observation: 'We have found a strange footprint on the shores of the unknown. We have devised profound theories, one after another, to account for its origins. At last, we have succeeded in reconstructing the creature that made the footprint. And lo! It is our own.' This may seem like an amusing or simplistic image, but it is in fact true. No one can deny the major impact of the development of space technology by humans and their societies since the 1960s. Yet rather than making Tsiolkovski's prophecy come true and bringing humanity far from its earthly

---

Esprit, January 1993, p. 138-139.
16. Jürgen Habermas, *La technique et la science comme "idéologie"*, Paris, NRF-Gallimard, 1973 (1968), p. 88-89.

roots, Sputnik and its successors have released these bonds only to replace them by even stronger ones. Never before has humankind been more attached to Earth. The same can be said of the question of ethics which has emerged in this field of activities. Rooted in a mythological, symbolic and philosophical or even theological tradition dating back to antiquity, the question of ethics demands nothing more than enhancing the strongest and most common of moral values: interest in the unknown, the will of power, the sense of responsibility, and the principle of vigilance, labour and fraternity. With this genealogy, the field of space ethics is by no means inferior to other supposedly more prestigious fields of ethics. On the contrary, it provides a unique horizon and one which is profoundly human—the horizon of space. In the way that it concentrates the world to the scale of humanity, and expands humanity to the scale of the world; space is no less than a new and unique humanist enterprise.

Sigillum Confessionis: The Seal Of Confession In Today's Roman Catholic Church

Robert Crotty
University of South Australia

Introduction

There is trouble, real trouble between Church and State, brewing in Australia over the issue of the Seal of Confession (known officially in Latin as *Sigillum Confessionis*), as maintained by the Roman Catholic Church, in regard to child abuse.

The reason that this matter has come to the fore is the calling by the then Prime Minister of Australia, on November 12 2012, of a Royal Commission into Institutional Responses to Child Sexual Abuse. Gillard, on April 3 2013 said that it would be 'an important moral moment for our nation'. The Commission held a preliminary meeting on that same day but there will be many more. At least 5000 alleged victims are expected to be heard. While an interim Report will be posted in 2014, the Final Report will not be drafted until 2015.

All institutions that have had custody of children in Australia will be scrutinised. However, while there are confirmed reports of widespread historical institutional abuse, the Roman Catholic Church is expected to be the main player among the accused. The Survivors' Network of Those Abused by Priests is adamant that the time has come for the Catholic Church to cease obfuscation and admit without equivocation what happened in the past.

While the Royal Commission (and some other State enquiries) will not solely examine the Roman Catholic Church, the Commission's membership should be aware that there is a dire problem that has been adumbrated but never, to my knowledge, fully explained. It is the intention of this article not to comment on the Royal Commission's procedures but on one aspect where, as I have said, I see trouble brewing. This regards the Seal of Confession.

Nicola Roxon, former Federal Attorney General, stated to ABC News 24 on 24 November 2012 that the forthcoming Royal Commission into child sex abuse will require Catholic priests to break the Seal of Confession in the matter of serious sexual offences.

> Child sex abuse is a crime, it should be reported, and I know that the royal commission is going to have some very complex issues to deal with

The next day the NSW Premier, Barry O'Farrell, a Catholic, told AM that a Catholic priest who hears a pedophile's confession should be subject to mandatory reporting.

> I think the law of the land when it comes to mandatory reporting around issues to do with children should apply to everyone equally,
> How can you possibly, by the continuation of this practice, potentially continue to give . . . a free pass to people who've engaged in the most heinous of acts?

Then Federal Liberal frontbencher, Christopher Pyne, who is also a Catholic, claimed that criminal law should take priority over church rules when it comes to child abuse. He told ABC News:

> If a priest hears in a confessional a crime, especially a crime against a minor, the priest has the responsibility in my view to report that to the appropriate authorities.

Then Opposition Leader Tony Abbott had backed the idea of requiring priests to reveal what they have heard in confession, saying there are already various legal requirements on people if they become aware of sexual offences against children. He told an ABC reporter in Brisbane:

> The law is no respecter of persons - everyone has to obey the law, regardless of what job they're doing, regardless of what position they hold.

Asked if that included priests as well, Mr Abbott replied: 'Indeed'.

Prior to the call for the Commission, there had been explosive allegations of cover-up by the Catholic Church with regard to pedophile priests. Both Roxon and Gillard made it clear that the Royal Commission would have a wider remit than the Catholic Church. The inquiry would cover the abuse of children in *all* Australian institutions. Gillard has taken a more cautious approach towards the particular problem regarding the Catholic Church, simply saying that the Royal Commission will need to consider the Seal of Confession.

In a very sincere but rather tortured article in the online *Eureka Street* on January 13, 2013, Bishop Geoffrey Robinson, a former Catholic auxiliary bishop of Sydney, wrote:

> I pray sincerely that I never face a situation where I was convinced that an innocent minor would be abused unless I broke the seal. I believe I would find it impossibly difficult to live with that abuse on my conscience.

Presumably, that is a vote against the Seal.

The Seal of Confession is not easy to understand. It has had a long history in the Roman Catholic Church and that history brings up some of the more pertinent issues involved in the present discussion. That history indeed explains why there can be no happy outcome from this impasse between Church and State.

I should make it clear that the purpose of this article is not to attack or defend the Seal of Confession as taught by the Catholic Church, and my own attitude is irrelevant apart from my intention to be objective. The purpose of the article is simply to indicate that some of the solutions (as portrayed in the political comment above), to what must become a serious obstacle to the Royal Commission, are simplistic and do not take account of the mindset of the Catholic Church.

The Sacrament of Penance

The private confession of sins to a Catholic priest by Catholic penitents, known as the Sacrament of Penance, and The Sacrament of Penance and Reconciliation in the parlance of more recent times, was not always a ritual within the Church. This is an historical fact which goes counter to the Church teaching that Jesus himself instituted the seven Catholic sacraments. This claim of Jesus' institution of The Sacrament of Penance was formally affirmed by Pius X in 1907 in a Syllabus of condemned errors called *Lamentabili*. The *error* that it solemnly condemned reads:

> The words of the Lord, "Receive the Holy Spirit; whose sins you shall forgive, they are forgiven them; and whose sins you shall retain, they are retained (John 20:22–23), in no way refer to the Sacrament of Penance, in spite of what it pleased the Fathers of Trent to say (Error 47).

Because of their alleged institution by Jesus, and the affirmation of this in later Church events like the Council of Trent, the seven Catholic sacraments are not mere ceremonials for true believers. For those who hold this position of faith, his institution makes them what they are as channels of divine grace to individuals. Accordingly, in Church teaching, the sacraments are not controlled by human whim or weakness. They are divinely constructed entities. If a sinful priest consecrates bread and wine into the body and blood of Jesus, then it works whether or not the priest is a fool or sinful. If an incompetent or sinful priest hears a confession and bestows absolution, then the absolution is valid.

What resources we have for tracing the sacramental practice of confession of sins in the history of the early Christian Church point, however, very clearly to a public ritual that did not develop until later when there was considerable Church organisation. The ritual was public and at times it seems to have been considered unrepeatable: the penitent had one chance to set matters aright. Some sins (such as heresy and murder) could never be forgiven. As part of a rather drawn-out ceremonial, those Church members who acknowledged themselves as, and were acknowledged to be, sinners were sequestered to a separate part of the church during religious services over a prolonged period of time. There would then be some form of general confession of sins and this would be followed eventually by a general absolution. This public ritual had other reasons for its perpetuation: it strengthened corporate identity and reconciled some community tensions.

Christian Ethics

The evolving practice of the sacrament of Penance followed the developing thought of the Church on religious Ethics. The early Christian church struggled to make sense of Ethics, the norms behind human patterns of behaviour. How can people ascertain what is right and what is wrong in human behaviour? Augustine of Hippo (354-430) supported the Natural Law theory (based on the cosmic order of the universe, and that order realised within each human - see Arntz, 1965: 23–32) which he developed from the writings of Plato and the works of Roman Stoics (Deman, 1951; Murphy, 1963: 49–85).

Plato's theory of Ideas had led the philosopher to claim that, from the experience of beautiful things, the human mind could perceive the Idea of the Beautiful and from the experience of good things the mind could apprehend the Idea of Goodness. The Stoics identified this Idea of Goodness with The Logos which permeated the universe. The Stoics added that humans shared in The Logos in a special way. Both Plato and the Stoics recognised that there was Nature and there was human reason. Reason tried to understand and apply the Ideas, but there was no guarantee that it could succeed. Nor was there any guarantee that human law reflected the Ideas. Nature was permanent and non-human; law was determined by human agreement, it was transitory.

Augustine claimed that the biblical idea of The Logos ('The Logos became flesh' as in John chapter 1) could well fit in with what became known as the *ius naturale* or the Natural Law. This Natural Law had been succinctly summarised for human usage in the Ten Commandments of the Hebrew Scriptures. Accordingly, those who followed Augustine's thinking, including for some centuries most of the intelligentsia of the Church, saw Christian Ethics as cut and dried. The way humans should respond to the requirements of God was predetermined. Humans could work out what should be done and what should be avoided. If there was ignorance or uncertainty about what was required in human action or if there was unwillingness to fulfil the demands, then these failings were due to Original Sin, the initial mind-clouding misdemeanour of Adam and Eve.

Thomas Aquinas (1225–1274) was to take up Augustine's teaching and develop it further. Earlier, the term *lex aeterna* had been used to cover both the Natural Law (which was applied to non-humans) and the *lex gentium* or Law of the Peoples (applied to humans) (Aubert, 1955: 93). Aquinas used the term *lex aeterna* to define the supreme form of all law. It was made identical with God.

Therefore, according to Aquinas, the *lex aeterna* directed the very nature of unthinking immaterial things towards their specific purpose in being. Humans, on the other hand, had reason and had the ability to consciously participate in the *lex aeterna*. This participation was the Natural Law.

> The light of natural reason which enables us to distinguish between good and evil – which belongs to the Natural Law—is nothing but the imprint of the divine light in us'. (*Summa Theologiae*, Ia IIae, q. 90, art.2, ad 1).

As far as the content of ethical demands went, Aquinas maintained that all humans could apprehend the basic ethical norm: Good must be done and Evil must be avoided. The conclusions that derived from this rational activity had been conveniently expanded in the Ten Commandments.

The difference in Aquinas' teaching is basically due to the fact that he saw the universe from an Aristotelian viewpoint, not Platonic or Stoic. For Augustine, Nature or reality was out there, beyond human ken. Humans tried by reason to understand this reality but might not succeed. For Aristotle, on the other hand, reality is what confronted the human mind. The Ideas of Plato were not real, not out there; they were categories that the mind used to order Nature. Reason and Nature were for Aristotle in perfect harmony. The primary conclusions of the Natural Law were naturally available to all humanity (Van Oberbeke, 1957: 75).

Ethics by this time had become absolutist (see Crotty, 2013). In fact, the Natural Law theogy was the most enduring presentation of absolutist Ethics even to the present day. During the Middle Ages this development in the understanding of Ethics had its effect on the Sacrament of Penance. According to the Natural Law theory, all sins could be recognised as such. Human reason was capable of understanding the Natural Law and to come to conclusions, even if there were seeming conflicts. On this basis, there were significant developments that would change it from a public ritual, performed infrequently, to a more individualistic confession of sins performed regularly.

Private Confession of Sins

The change began within Celtic Christianity where a new form of the ritual came into usage (Oakley, 1938: 147–164 and 581–601; Bierler (ed), 1963; Charles-Edwards, 2000). This is not the place to argue the matter here, but the Celtic Church seems never to have separated from Rome, as many have argued, and it seems that, in general, like the rest of Western Christians, members of Celtic Christianity acknowledged the primacy of Rome (Davies, 1992). However, like most other distant sections of the Christian world, given little possibility of central oversight, it developed its own Christian practices and beliefs (Corning, 2006: 2–4).

One novel practice was the private confession of sins (McNeil and Gamer, 1938: 7–17). The practice began as a monastic custom, monasteries being a feature of Celtic Christianity, and the custom spread to the Celtic laity. The confession was made to a priest with the security of the seal of secrecy. A penance was decided on by the confessor and this was performed privately by the penitent.

Because of this link forged between the particular type of a sin and its due penance, there was the production from the sixth century of *Libri Poenitentiales*, Penitential Books, handbooks that listed, in due order, particular sins and an appropriate penance for each. The sins and their penances were based on any indications regarding penances for particular sins in the text of the Bible, on particular extant canons in Church Law, on particular practices within monasteries and finally on the personal judgement of leaders within the Celtic monastic movement.

When Irish missionaries went into Europe they brought this practice of private Confession with them (Vogel, 1952; Corning, 2006: 18). Use of public penance had been declining in Europe. Thus, Columbanus (543–615), a famous Irish missionary who travelled widely in Gaul and Italy to establish Celtic monasteries, was credited with recharging European Christianity and, in particular, was described as introducing the *medicamenta paenitentiae*, the 'medicines of penance', into Gaul (Brown, 2003: 252). However, there was no widespread uptake of this new practice of private confession and the attendant use of the Penitential Books. It was said, against the Books, that they did not have any authority from the Church, that there were discrepancies between one and another and that some of the personal penances imposed were suspect, particularly those that did not involve giving alms to the Church.

The Seal of Confession

It is in conjunction with this practice of a private confession of sins to a confessor, with the attribution of a fitting penance, that the Seal of Confession can be found. Secrecy was part of the Celtic practice; it continued when the confession of sins moved to Europe. The Seal of Confession consists in the absolute duty of priests not to disclose, directly or indirectly, anything that they might learn from penitents during the course of the Sacrament of Penance. It has always been an absolutist duty; there could be no exceptions or interpretations. It applies to both direct disclosure, where the offending priest would communicate what he has heard in confession to another, and indirect disclosure, where the offending priest would change his manner of speech or action according to what he had heard during the confession.

The obligation and the penalties incurred by breaking that obligation outweighed any other form of professional secrecy (for example, that of a doctor or lawyer). The priest could not therefore break the seal in order to save his own life or the life of another, to refute a false accusation (one of Hitchcock's films *I Confess* was based on this assumption: a murderer confesses to a priest and then frames him for the murder), to avert a public catastrophe or to forward the cause of justice.

One of the earliest compilations of Church Law (drawn up from edicts of General Councils and existing Church law) was made by the jurist, Gratian. Little is known of him; he flourished in the twelfth century CE but his full name and exact movements are in doubt. His principal work was called the *Decretum* and published about 1151. It tried to coordinate many collections of Church law, among them early statements on the Seal of Confession:

> Let the priest who dares to make known the sins of his penitent be deposed.

Gratian goes on to declare that anyone breaking the Seal should be deemed an ignominious wanderer for the rest of his life.

But the turning point in instituting the practice of private confession of sins and the Seal of Confession came in the thirteenth century. In 1215 there was a General Council held in Rome, Lateran IV. Amongst much else, it dealt with the Sacrament of Penance, in the form of a private confession of sins, defending its usage against 'heretics' who contradicted it and against abuses that had already been encountered in administering the sacrament. This was the first time that the Sacrament of Penance was dealt with comprehensively by a formal Church body. It advocated the obligation for all Catholics to confess their sins at least once a year. Very importantly for our discussion, at the same time it made a declaration on the Seal of Confession:

> Let the priest absolutely beware that he does not by word or sign or by any manner whatever in any way betray the sinner: but if he should happen to need wiser counsel let him cautiously seek the same without any mention of person. For whoever shall dare to reveal a sin disclosed to him in the tribunal of penance We decree that he shall be not only deposed from the priestly office but that he shall also be sent into the confinement of a monastery to do perpetual penance. (Canon 21).

Confession of sins and Seal of Confession were inextricably linked by the Conciliar statements. For the Roman Catholic Church God's revelation to humanity is achieved not only by means of the Scriptures but also by Tradition. Tradition includes the formal statements of Councils and Popes whereby they explicate what might be implicit in the Scriptures. The Roman Catholic Church to this day is bound by the Seal of Confession, as if it were explicitly written into the Scriptures.

Later Developments

After Lateran IV a new literary genre emerged, the *Summa de Casibus Poenitentiae* or Summary of Cases of Penance (see Michaud-Quantin, 1962). These books were meant to help priests in their duties as confessors by identifying all manner of sinfulness and they reflected the debates about Ethics that continued in the universities. These *Summae* intended to ensure that the confessors interrogated their penitents 'distinctly and methodically' about the exact nature of their sins. Guidelines were established: common sins that should be investigated could be identified in the Ten Commandments, next in the list of Seven Deadly Sins, and also in the lists of perceived abuses of each of the five human senses. Once a sin had been identified in its proper category it was laid down that no further details should be elicited from the penitent, particularly where sexual sins were being confessed.

Public confession of sins may not have been rendered redundant immediately. There is evidence that public penitential rituals continued in parts of France, and possibly elsewhere even after Lateran IV (Mansfield, 2005). However, by at least the sixteenth century only the private confession of sins was known in the Roman Catholic Church.

What had happened was that the medieval Church had accepted the Natural Law theory in some form. By reference to this it was claimed that any case of conscience, where there was doubt as to the sinful character of a behaviour, could be eventually solved as to its licitness or illicitness. This judgement was basically the preserve of the ordained clergy who, in this case, instead of acting as priests or teachers, acted as judges. As judges, they had the concomitant obligation of maintaining the Seal of Confession.

Church law had long been in a mess by the twentieth century. After several years of intense labour, the *Code of Canon Law* was published in 1917, and then edited in a revised edition in 1983. Both compilations have insisted on the Seal of Confession and dealt with the penalty for its abrogation: immediate on-the-spot excommunication from the Church, which could be lifted only by recourse to the Pope (Canon 1456.1 in the 1917 version and Canon 983.1 and 1388.1 in the 1983 version).

The Casuists

Legal casuists within the Church have considered all circumstances surrounding cases of dispute linked to the Seal of Confession. Catholic jurists have ventured to say that, for a very compelling reason, the priest can reveal to another what was said, but the penitent must have earlier given clear permission and, even in this case, the identity of the person could never be revealed.

The casuists have debated about the confessed sin being made available to civil authorities. While it has been considered that the priest could encourage penitents to hand themselves over to the legal authority, in cases where a sin is clearly also illegal (and this would manifestly include child abuse), in no case could the priest, either directly or indirectly, inform the authorities of the sin himself.

What appears from this historical review is that the Roman Catholic Church will never give in on this matter. The Seal of Confession, as it stands in Canon Law, is absolute and inviolate. Both the ritual of Penance and, as has been revealed for Catholics in the sacred Tradition of the Church, the Seal of Confession were set up by Jesus himself. A priest would be required to suffer imprisonment, torture or execution rather than break the Seal. If, hypothetically, the Canon Law on this matter were to be repealed, then the whole history of the implementation of this sacrament would need to be reviewed. In strict Roman Catholic teaching, this cannot be done. If Jesus actually instituted the sacrament, even if its actual praxis including the Seal took some time to come into full operation, then it cannot be altered or repealed. New liturgical forms of the Sacrament might be allowed, such as the three forms promulgated by Paul VI in 1973. However, even in the two more public of these forms, private confession of sins would be required at some time. In whatever case, the content of the confession of sins would remain perpetually under the Seal.

This would seem to be an immovable obstacle, counter to a search for information in the matter of the pedophile's confession of child abuse. The Australian Catholic Church has proposed a number of ways in which the debate might be moved forward. Cardinal George Pell has repeated adamantly that the Seal of Confession is inviolable. That would seem to be the end of the matter from his point of view. However, he then went on to argue that if a priest should know a penitent was a sexual abuser then he should refuse to hear the confession. It is not clear how this could be achieved in practice, or whether it is a valid response from the Catholic viewpoint.

What would it mean for a priest to refuse to hear the sins of a known pedophile, priest or not? The same Code of Canon Law that protects the Seal of Confession also protects Catholics who would confess their sins. The Code clearly states that all Catholics have the right to confess their sins, even horrific sins such as child abuse (canons 213, 843, 991). In fact, they have an obligation to do so (canons 988-989) and must confess their sins at least once a year. Further, they have a right to absolution of these sins if they are penitent (canon 980). Hence, the Pell solution would not seem to be lawful, under the present canonical structure or any foreseeable restructure.

Another suggested remedy has been for confessors to only give absolution to a pedophile on the condition that the pedophile reports the offence to civil authorities. We can compare this to the case where the confessor hears the confession of a person who has stolen a large amount of money. The absolution is made conditional on the penitent's intention to make reparation and return the money. However, in this case the priest cannot delay absolution until the reparation has been made. It is bestowed immediately. If subsequently the penitent decides not to make reparation, then another and separate sin has been committed. The priest may never be aware of this transgression. Even if he did become aware, he would still be bound by the Seal of Confession. The confessor cannot take it on himself to inform the authorities or make known the sin of theft.

The same is true of the absolution of a pedophile. It is not clear that requiring the pedophile to contact the civil authorities could ever become a canonical requirement (the penitent thief is not bound to report a theft, even a large one, only to make reparation which can be done in secret and complete anonymity). So long as the penitent pedophile indicates that the present intention is to avoid the sin in the future (with the ever-present possibility of recidivism), then the pedophile must be absolved and the confessor is bound thereafter by the Seal of Confession.

Conclusion

This article was never intended to solve the problem of the Seal of Confession as it will probably raise its head in the course of the Royal

Commission. Nor was it meant to comment on the Commission and its workings. It was intended to show that, in one potential matter that will undoubtedly raise its head during the Commission, we are not dealing with the situation of a doctor whose patient has a communicable disease or of a lawyer who has become aware that a client is a dangerous psychopath. The Catholic Church has forged a serious social problem for itself with the Seal of Confession. From the point of view of the historian, the matter is caught up with a series of events and circumstances that brought about the practice of the Seal. For the Roman Catholic Church the matter is part of the divine, eternal and immutable order of things. The Seal of Confession has been welded into Catholic Church law and practice related to the confession of sins as instituted by Jesus himself in such a way that only an amendment to the Church's divine constitution could allow that Seal to be broken.

This would mean questioning Jesus' institution of the Sacrament in its present form (and Pius X has made it clear that the Scriptures fully substantiate that institution), radically changing a divinely instituted practice, abrogating the decrees of the Lateran IV Ecumenical Council, rejecting binding papal pronouncements since that time and amending the Code of Canon Law.

That is not going to happen.

Bibliography

Arntz, J. (1965), 'Natural Law and its History', *Concilium*, 5, pp. 23-32

Aubert, J. (1955), *Le droit romain dans l'oeuvre de Saint Thomas*, Vrin: Paris

Bieler, L. (1963), *The Irish Penitentials* (5 vols), Dublin Institute for Advanced Studies: Dublin

Brown, P., (2003), *The Rise of Christendom*, sec. ed., Blackwell: Oxford.

Charles-Edwards, T. (2000), *Early Christian Ireland*, CUP: Cambridge,

Corning, C. (2006), *The Celtic and Roman Traditions: Conflict and Consensus in the Early Medieval Church*, Macmillan: London

Crotty, R. (2013), 'Human and Religious Values. A Relativistic Perspective' in Arthur, J. & Lovat, T. (eds.), *Handbook of Religion and Values*. Routledge: London

Davies, W. (1992), 'The Myth of the Celtic Church' in N. Edwards and A. Lane (eds.), *The Early Church in Wales and the West*, Oxford: Oxbow, pp. 12-21

Deman, T. (1951), *Aux origins de la theologie morale*, Institut d'études médiévales: Paris

Mansfield, M. (2005), *The Humiliation of Sinners: Public Penance in Thirteenth Century France*, Ithaca: Cornell University Press.

McNeil, J. and Gamer, H. (eds) (1938), *Medieval Handbooks of Penance*, Columba University Press: New York

Michaud-Quantin, P. (1962), *Sommes de casuistique et manuels du confession au moyen age (XII-XVI siecles), Analecta Mediaevalia Namurcensia*, 13, Nauwelaets: Louvain

Murphy, F.X. (1963), 'The Background to a History of Patristic Moral Thought', *Studia Moralia 1*, pp. 48-85

Oakley, T. (1938), 'Celtic Penance. Its Sources, Affiliation and Influence', *Irish Ecclesiastical Review*, 52, pp. 147-164

Van Oberbeke, P. (1957), 'Loi naturel et droit naturel selon S. Thomas', *Revue Thomiste*, 57, pp. 53-78

Vogel, C. (1952), *La discipline penitentielle en Gaule des origins à la fin du VIIe siècle*, Letouzey et Ain: Paris

CPSIA information can be obtained at www.ICGtesting.com
Printed in the USA
BVOW02*2044170316

440299BV00010B/10/P